# THE PRICE SPIRAL METHOD

# THE PRICE SPIRAL METHOD

## BY
## B.J. HOWARD

WINDSOR BOOKS, BRIGHTWATERS, NEW YORK

Published by Windsor Books
P.O. Box 280
Brightwaters, N.Y., 11718

Manufactured in the United States of America

ISBN 0-930233-32-8

**CAVEAT:** It should be noted that all commodity trades, patterns, charts, systems, etc., discussed in this book are for illustrative purposes only and are not to be construed as specific advisory recommendations. Further note that no method of trading or investing is foolproof or without difficulty, and past performance is no guarantee of future performance. All ideas and material presented are entirely those of the author and do not necessarily reflect those of the publisher or bookseller.

*This Book is Dedicted*
*to*
*My Father*

*Lloyd C. Clairmont*

# TABLE OF CONTENTS

# Preface

This book is the outcome of many hours spent in the research and development of a system that would "work" for any time period, and yet not become so technical as to render it beyond the understanding of the average individual. I have read many books on the stock market which either made little sense, were full of inconsistencies, or proved faulty when put into actual use.

During the course of developing my Price Spiral Method, I picked several past markets to "test" my system on before being satisfied that indeed it does work. It requires only a small amount of your time to keep it updated, and the *only* information needed is the closing price each day of the Dow Jones Industrials, or of any stock or commodity you wish to follow. These closing prices are published daily in most large newspapers throughout the country.

I have divided this book into three parts: Part 1 deals with the mathematical basis behind this system, and offers an explanation of *why* this method works. Part 2 explains in detail the complete Price Spiral Method and how it is used to track both a Bull Market and a Bear Market from start to finish. Part 3 is *unique* in itself in that it has *never before been published* in any book or article. It contains charts covering each and every Bull and Bear Market over the past 177 years, with charts illustrating all the Intermediate waves for each market for the past 88 years. These charts will prove to be a *most* valuable reference section.

# Part 1
# THE FOUNDATION BASICS

# The Foundation Basics

The Fibonacci Summation Series was introduced in 1201, by the Italian mathematician Leonardo Fibonacci (pronounced Fi-bo-na'-chee) in his book Liber Abacci ("a book about the abacus"). This contained the algebra and arithmetic he had assimilated during his travels to Greece, Egypt, Sicily, and Syria. His book played a notable part in the development of mathematics in Western Europe in subsequent centuries. In particular, Fibonacci showed that the Roman numeral system was inferior to the decimal place notation of the Hindus and Arabs.

The basis of the Fibonacci Summation Series is: the sum of any two adjacent numbers in the sequence forms the next highest number in the sequence. Therefore, 1 plus 1 equals 2, 1 plus 2 equals 3, 2 plus 3 equals 5, 3 plus 5 equals 8, 5 plus 8 equals 13, etc. etc. Starting with the number 1, the series develops as follows: 1, 1, 2, 3, 5, 8, 13, 21, 34, 55, 89, 144, 233...stretching on into infinity.

The ratio of any number to the next highest number is approximately 1.618 and the ratio of any number to the next lowest number is .618. These ratios are called PHI.

In the nineteenth century a French mathematician, E. Lucas, introduced the Lucas Numbers, which are closely related to the Fibonacci numbers. The numbers in the Lucas sequence are 1, 3, 4, 7, 11, 18, 29, 47...etc. This Lucas sequence is formed in the exact manner as the Fibonacci sequence. The sum of any two adjacent numbers in the sequence forms the next highest number.

Lucas also derived the equation for Divine Proportion:

$$(a/b \text{ equals } b/(a+b) \text{ where } a<b, \times \text{ equals } b/a).$$

This states that any line can be divided in such a way that the ratio between the smallest part (S) and the largest part (L) is equal to the ratio between the larger part (L) and the whole (W), and this ratio is always 1.618 (and .618).

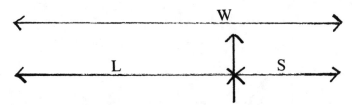

The equation for Divine Proportion yields the *Golden Section;*

$$\text{PHI equals } (\sqrt{5}+1)/2 = 1.618$$
$$\text{PHI equals } (\sqrt{5}+3)/2 = 2.618$$
$$\text{PHI equals } (2\sqrt{5}+4)/2 = 4.236$$
$$\text{PHI equals } (3\sqrt{5}+7)/2 = 6.854$$
$$\text{PHI equals } (5\sqrt{5}+11)/2 = 11.090$$
$$\text{PHI equals } (8\sqrt{5}+18)/2 = 17.944$$
$$\text{PHI equals } (13\sqrt{5}+29)/2 = 29.0344$$

The above exhibits one of the many interrelationships between the Fibonacci and Lucas numbers. The 2, 3, 5, 8, and 13 terms in the equations are Fibonacci numbers, while the 3, 4, 7, 11, 18, and 29 terms are Lucas numbers.

While working with these basics for my Spiral Method, I have developed an equation which, to the best of my knowledge, has never before been employed. That equation is as follows:

$$L/2 + \sqrt{(L/2)^2 + L^2} = \underline{\text{W}} \quad \text{and} \quad L/2 - \sqrt{L/2^2 + L^2} = \underline{\text{S}}$$

**where**

W equals Whole

L = Larger    S = Smaller

Again the ratios involved in this "Golden Section" are 1.618 and .618. Using the above equation, the following TABLES are produced to EXACT proportion, correct to the **6th** decimal place.

| Larger L | $\sqrt{(L/2)^2 + L^2}$ | Whole + L/2 | Smaller − L/2 | W/L |
|---|---|---|---|---|
| | *Next L increasing value* | | | |
| 29.034442 | 32.461493 | 46.978718 | 17.944272 | 1.618034 |
| 17.944272 | 20.062306 | 17.944272 | 6.854102 | 1.618034 |
| 6.854102 | 7.663119 | 11.090170 | 4.236068 | 1.618034 |
| 4.236068 | 4.736068 | 6.854102 | 2.618034 | 1.618034 |
| 2.618034 | 2.927051 | 4.236068 | 1.618034 | 1.618034 |
| 1.618034 | 1.809017 | 2.618034 | 1.000000 | 1.618034 |
| 1.000000 | 1.118034 | 1.618034 | .618034 | 1.618034 |
| .618034 | .690983 | 1.000000 | .381966 | 1.618034 |
| .381966 | .427051 | .618034 | .236068 | 1.618034 |
| .236068 | .263932 | .381966 | .145898 | 1.618034 |
| .145898 | .1631189 | .236068 | .0901699 | 1.618034 |
| | *Next L decreasing value* | | | |

*Note:* The numbers in the L column, after 1.618034 in increasing values, are *exactly* the same if rounded off to the nearest whole number, as each and every number in the *Lucas Sequence!*

Now, using the Tables above we shall proceed to construct the Golden Rectangle. Using an L equal to 2.618034 as our line segment in our example, we first draw out a square, with all 4 sides equal to 2.618034 in length. Going across the Table, starting at the L (larger) column for our line segment of 2.618034, to the S (smaller) column we find the number 1.618034. We next *extend* the top and bottom lines on our square out to equal an extension of 1.618034. Draw another line on the right side to connect the newly extended top and bottom (the length of this line is, of course, equal to the line at the left, 2.618034 in height). At this point we have a Golden Rectangle as shown in the figure on the following page.

**Figure 1**
**Golden Rectangle**

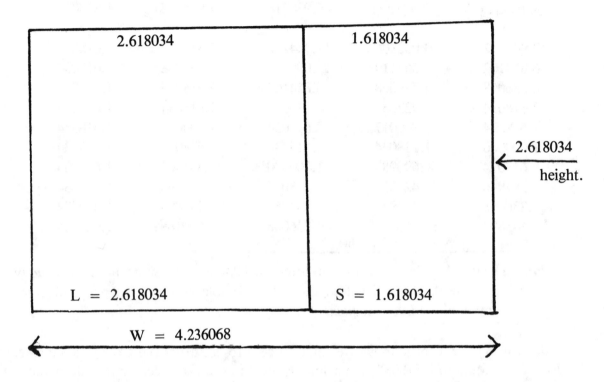

Continuing on, we next divide the right hand rectangle into yet another Golden Rectangle. Our new L now becomes 1.618034, again going across from an L of 1.618034 to the S (smaller) column. We see that we draw our next line from top to bottom, dividing the segment into an L of 1.618034, and an S of 1.000000. S now becomes our new L. Going across to the S column we find that we divide this new rectangle at an S of exactly .618034, and draw a line from top to bottom. Since the S of .618034 now becomes our new L, we go across to the S column and see that S now equals .381966. Again we divide this new rectangle at exactly that point by drawing a line from top to bottom.

We could go on and on, dividing up a new and smaller rectangle each time, but for our purpose we can stop here at 5 divisions. We have constructed the original Golden Rectangle (Figure 1) and divided it up into 4 more Golden Rectangles, each of smaller dimensions, creating like from like, as represented in the figure on the next page.

## FOUR GOLDEN RECTANGLES

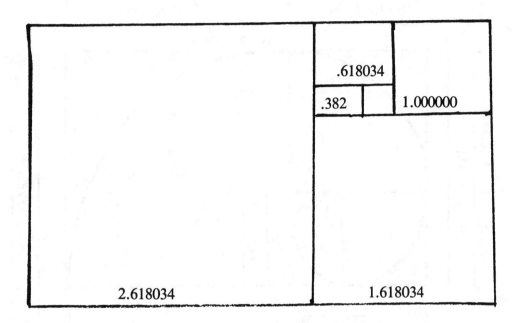

**Figure 2**

We could have started with any line segment and expanded by using the W column for our new L. Or we could have decreased our Golden Rectangle by using the S column for our new L to absolutely perfect proportions and with ratios of exactly 1.618034 to .618034.

Now we are ready to add the Spiral to the Golden Rectangle we just constructed. Simply draw a curve from one line intersection to the next as shown on the next page.

## ADDING LOGARITHMIC SPIRAL TO THE GOLDEN RECTANGLE

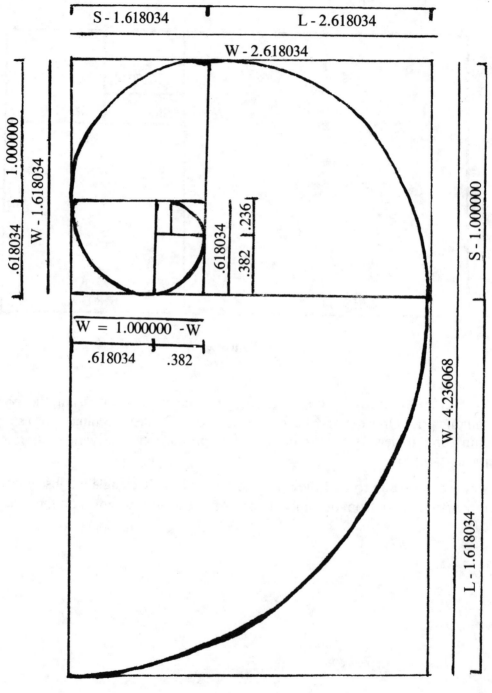

**Figure 3**

Nonlinear mathematics consolidates the elements of energy, stability, instability, and dynamic wave form to describe the economy. This is used in many fields, such as physical and biological science, engineering and electronics, just to name a few.

Lets define the concept of stability:

Instantaneous Balanced Stability = a minimum or maximum of Potential Energy.

**Figure 5**
**INSTANTANEOUS BALANCED STABILITY**

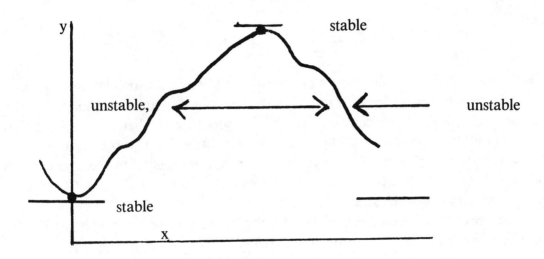

There are resistant forces called "damping" that act to reduce the energy of a system in motion, eventually bringing it to a position of balance and momentary stop (the stable condition).

Resistance is proportional to velocity, increasing as magnitude increases, until they become fairly equal. A resistant force that opposes the motion of a system will have a direction opposite that of the system's velocity.

Therefore, in any unstable oscillation (or wave) the amplitude will increase or decrease depending on whether E or E-d is dominating.

Where: E = energy present, and E-d = loss of energy due to damping.

The combination of E and E-d results in a wave form as depicted in the figure on the following page.

### The Combination of Energy and the Damping Effect

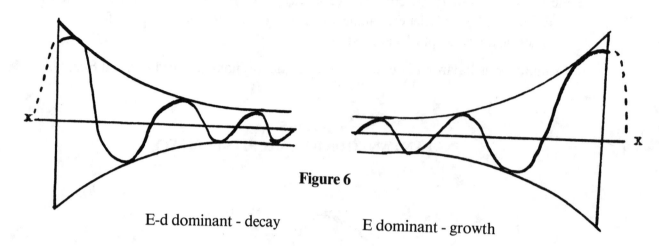

**Figure 6**

E-d dominant - decay          E dominant - growth

It is further stated, in the text books on the subject of nonlinear oscillations, that the energy of a system decays logarithmically with time as a system amplitude falls off. Since the "damping" which causes the decay is proportional, then so too does the growth or amplitude increase logarithmically. We shall prove this theorem shortly.

The Logarithmic Spiral is one of a family of trajectories related to the stability (or instability) of cycles and wave forms, and deals with the existence of "Limit Cycles or circles" in which a Logarithmic Spiral unfolds.

In the study of limit cycles it is stated that *if* the logarithmic spiral crosses the X axis more than *three* times, then at least two limit cycles exist.

Let us take the Logarithmic Spiral we previously constructed and inscribe our rotations of the spiral into one Limit Circle as shown in the figure below. Note that we have marked the 3 crossings of the x axis, showing that only one cycle is present, and we have also put each rotation (wave) into its proper quadrant. Each 90 degree rotation on the curve *should* generate a wave.

### Limit Circle With Logarithmic Spiral
#### Figure 7

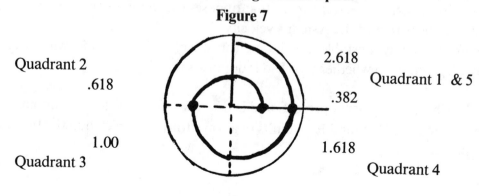

Quadrant 2

.618

2.618

Quadrant 1 & 5

.382

1.00

Quadrant 3

1.618

Quadrant 4

**Figure 8**

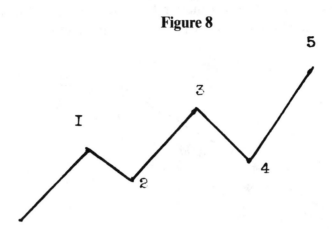

Now, let's prove that indeed this Logarithmic Spiral does grow and at the same time decay proportionally, at a *logarithmic* rate. Also, we'll prove that it is necessary to "change" the 90 degree rotations slightly to achieve not only the wave form in Figure 8, but also the proportion for growth and decay it contains.

We are going to construct a chart for our Spiral values, which will be labeled Y.

X equals 1.618
t equals time 1, 2, 3, 4, 5.

$e^a$ equals LOG. of 1.618,       = .208970517
$e^b$ equals LOG. of 90 Degrees,  = 1.9542425

| t | X | Rectangular Coordinates | Y | Polar Coordinates |
|---|---|---|---|---|
| 1. | −2. | $X * e^a$ = invert LOG. = | .382 | $t + e^b$ = inv. LOG. = 90° |
| 2. | −1. | $X * e^a$ = invert LOG. = | .618 | $t + e^b$ = inv. LOG. = 180° |
| 3. | 0. | $X * e^a$ = invert LOG. = | 1.000 | $t + e^b$ = inv. LOG. = 270° |
| 4. | 1. | $X * e^a$ = invert LOG. = | 1.618 | $t + e^b$ = inv. LOG. = 360° |
| 5. | 2. | $X * e^a$ = invert LOG. = | 2.618 | $t + e^b$ = inv. LOG. = 450° |

Using the table we calculated on the previous page, just as it is, I'll illustrate the wave form. Time will remain the same no matter how we rearrange the y values for our Spiral. Therefore, the polar coordinates will also remain the same.

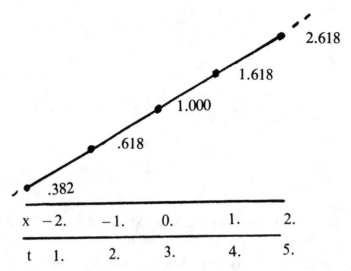

Clearly what we have here is a straight line growth, with no decay (damping). This is also a *1st Degree* polynomial, known as linear regression = 1 wave.

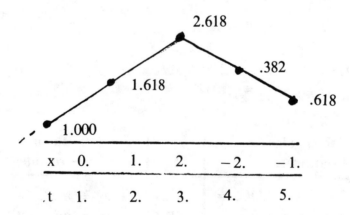

A 2nd Degree polynomial, giving us 2 waves, and a proportional decay rate.

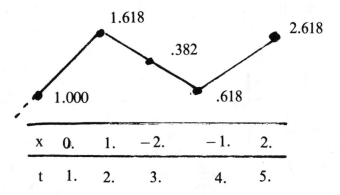

A 3rd Degree polynomial, giving us 3 waves, with proportional decay.

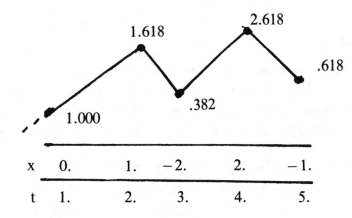

A 4th Degree polynomial equaling 4 waves, with proportional decay.

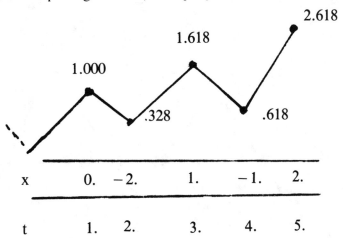

A 5th Degree polynomial—giving us the *5 wave form we were seeking,* and decay proportional to growth.

A computer run fitting the x and y data to a 5th degree polynomial curve fit yields the following:

| Coefficients | at x | y equals |
|---|---|---|
| 4.20672774E-07 | 0. | 0. |
| .999899237 | 1.    (x  0.) | .999998567 |
| 4.1950095E -04 | 382 (x − 2.) | .381997445 |
| − 5.68193411E-04 | 1.618 (x   1.) | 1.61800024 |
| 3.00858104E-04 | .618 (x − 1.) | .618003341 |
| − 5.32560443E-04 | 2.618 (x   2.) | 2.617999999 |

Goodness of fit 100%

A second computer run of the coefficients, to find the roots of our 5th degree polynomial, yielded the two roots, one positive and one negative. This is plotted below to clearly show the 5 crossings of the zero axis. This confirms that we are dealing with two cycles, or two forces here; one growth, the other decay.

Positive root:     .149455342
Negative root:   − .156185907

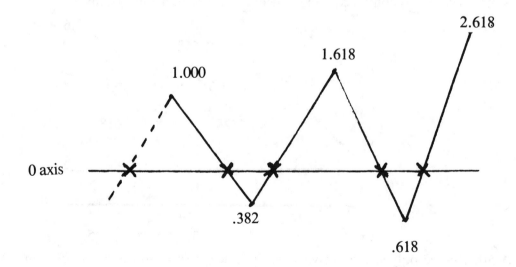

If we had wished to find the roots of our original Spiral, which was a 1st degree polynomial, we could have solved for this by using a quadratic equation:

| t | Y | Positive root | Negative root |
|---|---|---|---|
| 0 | .236 | | |
| 1. | .382 | .382/ .236 = 1.618 | − 1 = .618 |
| 2. | .618 | .618/ .382 = 1.618 | − 1 = .618 |
| 3. | 1.000 | 1.000/ .618 = 1.618 | − 1 = .618 |
| 4. | 1.618 | 1.618/1.000 = 1.618 | − 1 = .618 |
| 5. | 2.618 | 2.618/1.618 = 1.618 | − 1 = .618 |

Now that we have the 5-wave pattern derived from our original Logarithmic Spiral, let's discuss "extensions."

Since the Spiral's cycles were initiated by e (energy), momentum is present, and the Spiral's condition is termed unstable. The wave will continue to unfold until a damping effect occurs and momentum decreased to the point of stability, which forms a peak or bottom. The length of the wave depends on the intensity of the energy present and the point at which the damping occurs.

If the energy is strong enough, an "extension" can occur in one of the Thrust Waves (waves 1, 3, or 5 on up moves and waves A, C, and E in down moves, as will be discussed later on). A *clue* to this extension can be gained from Wave 6, as it will *not* exhibit the strong downward thrust of a normal A wave, and instead will resemble waves 2 and 4 in its sub-normal strength.

If an extension does occur, then the figure below shows how our Spiral extends and in what quadrants it falls.

**Figure 9**

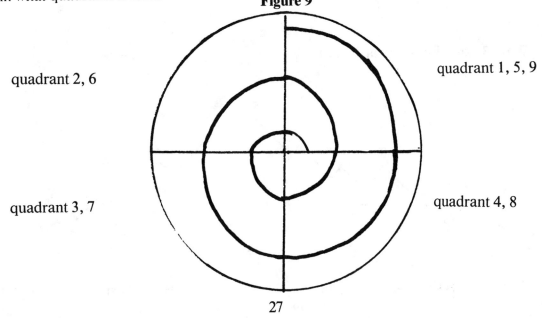

quadrant 2, 6

quadrant 1, 5, 9

quadrant 3, 7

quadrant 4, 8

27

Basic extension patterns in the total wave formations.

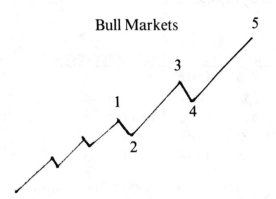

**Bull Markets**

Wave 1 extension—upward trend.

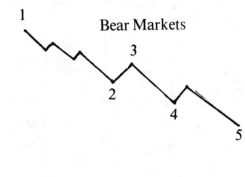

**Bear Markets**

Wave 1 extension—down trend.

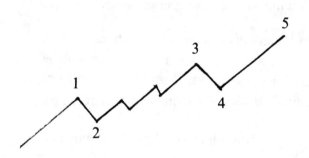

Wave 3 extension—upward trend.

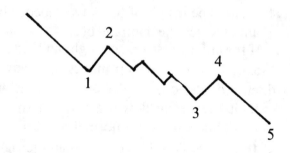

Wave 3 extension—down trend.

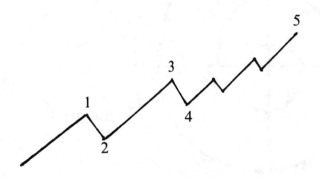

Wave 5 extension—upward trend.

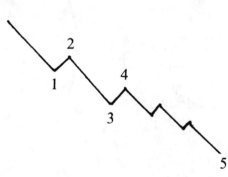

Wave 5 extension—down trend.

Before going on to a brief discussion of the Elliott Theory, I would like to add a few more rather interesting facts concerning the Fibonacci and Lucas number sequence, as well as the Golden Ratios of 1.618 and .618.

First of all, the following illustration does nothing more than show the "error" factor between the first 11 numbers of the Fibonacci sequence, until they converge to a ratio of 1.618.

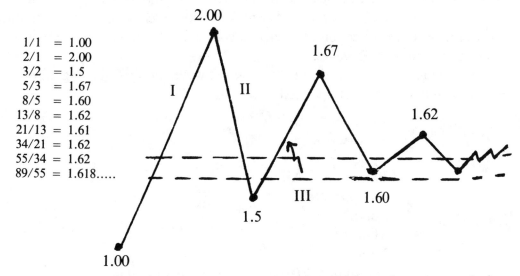

1/1  = 1.00
2/1  = 2.00
3/2  = 1.5
5/3  = 1.67
8/5  = 1.60
13/8  = 1.62
21/13 = 1.61
34/21 = 1.62
55/34 = 1.62
89/55 = 1.618.....

The error factor is due solely to rounding off the decimal side to the nearest whole number.

Both the Fibonacci and Lucas sequences can be calculated by the means of logarithmic tables or by calculator.

---

To calculate the *16th* number in the Fibonacci sequence, which is 987,

F. 16 = $\sqrt{5}$ = 2.2356304

Log. 2.2356304 = .3494

Log. 1.61803407 = .20898

*16* *.20898 minus .3494 = 2.9944016

Invert Log. 2.994016 = 987.19194 rounded off = 987.

---

AND

---

To calculate the *14th* number of the Lucas sequence, which is 843,

Log. 2.618034 = .20898

*14* * .20898 = 2.925827

Invert Log. 2.925827 = 842.99889 rounded off = 843.

---

Any other number in either sequence can be calculated by simply changing the *multiplier.* Note: The Lucas numbers are the easiest of the two sequences to calculate. Again I want to point out that the Lucas numbers, if *not* rounded off to the nearest whole number, are exactly the same as the expanding Golden Ratio's sequence.

We now come to a brief summarization of the works of Ralph Nelson Elliott and his Elliott Wave Theory. Basically, he founded this theory on the Fibonacci sequence, the Logarithmic Spiral, and the Golden Ratios of 1.618 and .618.

Elliott believed that the moves of Stock Market prices fluctuated in "natural ways," with moves in the direction of the trend containing 5 waves, and those in the opposite direction containing 3 waves.*

He listed names for the degree (or class) of waves in the following order, in reference to the length of time each spanned:

> Grand Supercycle
> Super Cycle
> Cycle
> Primary
> Intermediate
> Minor
> Minute
> Minuette
> Sub-minuette (found only in hourly data)

The basic patterns for the Primary, Intermediate, and the Minor are illustrated in the figure on the next page. These are the ones we are most concerned with, as they cover the Bull and Bear markets of approximately 2 years duration.

To the basic pattern, Elliott then attached many exceptions and variations, much too numerous and complex to explore here. Elliott had some difficulty in the application of his theories, in that some turning points were not "clear-cut." There seemed to be endless variations, making it quite difficult to grasp for the average person. The real problem here is one of interpretation.

With this background established, I can now proceed to the main reason for this book—to offer a simple, easy method that *anyone* can use to track each and every wave development in the Stock or Commodity Market. We will be using some of Elliott's Wave patterns, the Lucas and Fibonacci sequence and most surely the Golden Ratios of 1.618 and .618. These are all combined into one simple system, which I have called *"The Price Spiral Method."*

We are dealing with *two* distinct and different types of Stock Market moves, the Bull (up) and the Bear (down) Markets. Each type has its own characteristics, which will be handled in two sections, but the same principles and methods shall apply to both.

---

\* An excellent reference on this subject is *"The Elliott Wave Theory"* by Frost and Prechter, available from Windsor Books, Box 280, Brightwaters, N.Y. 11718.

**Figure 10**

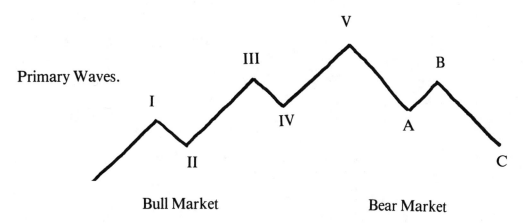

Primary Waves.

Bull Market          Bear Market

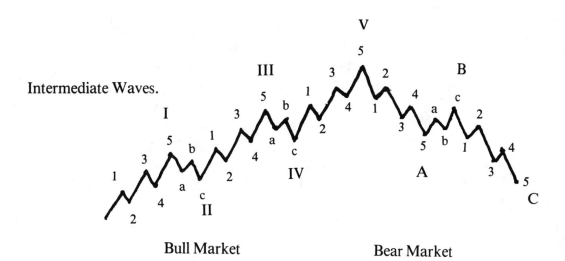

Intermediate Waves.

Bull Market          Bear Market

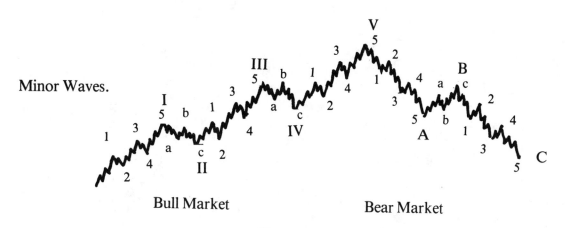

Minor Waves.

Bull Market          Bear Market

# Part II
# The Price Spiral Method

# The Price Spiral Method

The progression of prices, either up or down through the Golden Ratios of the Logarithmic Spiral, is the *key* to a highly accurate and simplified system, which I call "The Price Spiral Method." These ratios will be used as a tracking device for prices as they increase or decrease, and they will signal formation of a peak or bottom, thereby giving us our wave count.

To do this, we are going to convert our logarithmic spiral ratios (Figure 11) to *Dollar Value Ratios.* Simply move the decimal point 2 places to the right and put a $ (dollar sign) to the left of the converted ratio. For example, 382 becomes $38.00. Our ratios are now 100 times larger than before. The resulting Logarithmic Price Spiral (Figure 12) is still identical to the original spiral, as they both increase and decrease by 1.618 and .618. By using these ratios converted to dollar values, we obtain a very effective method of applying Elliott's Wave Theory to the Stock Market. We also don't have to interpret the very complex and numerous pattern variations associated with Elliott's method, because for the most part the Price Spiral Method will ignore them, until a definite move resumes, either up or down.

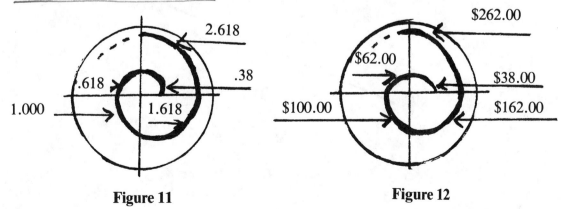

Figure 11                    Figure 12

35

## Chart For Converting Golden Ratios
## To Logarithmic Price Spiral Dollar Values

| Ratios | Dow & Higher Priced Stocks | Lower Priced Stocks |
|---|---|---|
| 6.854 | $685.00 | |
| 4.236 | $424.00 | |
| 2.618 | $262.00 | |
| $.618 | $162.00 | |
| 1.000 | $100.00 | $10.00 |
| .618 | $ 62.00 | $ 6.20 |
| .382 | $ 38.00 | $ 3.80 |
| .236 | $ 24.00 | $ 2.40 |
| .146 | $ 15.00 | $ 1.50 |
| .090 | $129.00 | $ .90 |
| .056 | $ 5.60 | $ .60 |
| .034 | $ 3.40 | $ .35 |
| .021 | $ 2.10 | $ .20 |

*Note:* Ratios can also be expanded to even greater amounts than listed (6.854) by simply multiplying the 6.854 by 1.618 to obtain the next highest ratio value, and repeating this process again with the new value. The larger dollar values calculated would be representative of Grand Super Cycles, or cycles covering longer time periods than one average Bull or Bear Market swing.

You may be wondering why we don't use the 5-wave pattern derived from the logarithmic spiral in Part I.

Well, the movement of the Stock Market prices is just never that clear cut and perfect. For example, the Bull Market of August 1982 to January 1984, which we shall be examining in detail shortly, had a Primary wave as follows:

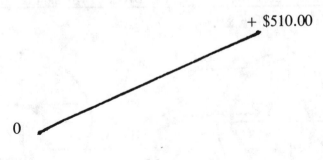

+ $510.00

0

The Intermediate 5-wave pattern within it looked like this:

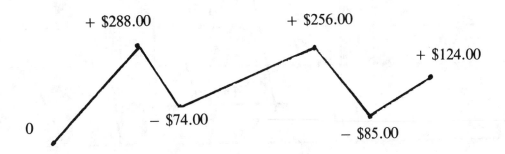

+ $288.00          + $256.00

+ $124.00

0          − $74.00          − $85.00

Plus, all the minor waves inside these waves exhibited irregular behavior. As you can see, actual price movement just doesn't quite *fit* our "Perfect Pattern" waves.

Here's where the Price Spiral Method comes in. For this market, we could see by looking at all 21 Minor Waves that the smallest wave equaled a $39.00 loss. We will use the ratio .382, now converted to a $38.00 dollar value, as our "starter" or base value (all moves *less* than $38.00 will be ignored) for our Logarithmic Price Spiral for Minor Waves. We'll just let "nature take its course" as we watch the wave unfold—*until* a move registers a *change of $38.00* in the opposite direction! This is our *signal* that a wave has ended and a new one is beginning.

For our Intermediate Wave Spiral, we see that the smallest wave was a $74.00 down move, so we would use the ratio .618, now $62.00, as our "starter" for the Intermediate Logarithmic Spiral. We will ignore all moves less than $62.00 (or *all* the Minor Wave Down moves) giving us a nice smooth line up and down to a 5-wave total.

(I'm *sure* you are wondering, *how* do we know what "starters" to use if the wave hasn't begun yet—I'll explain how easy it is, in just a short while).

In effect, we really are using our "Perfect 5-Wave Pattern" from Part I. Just remember, it can rearrange itself into one of *six* variations as shown...

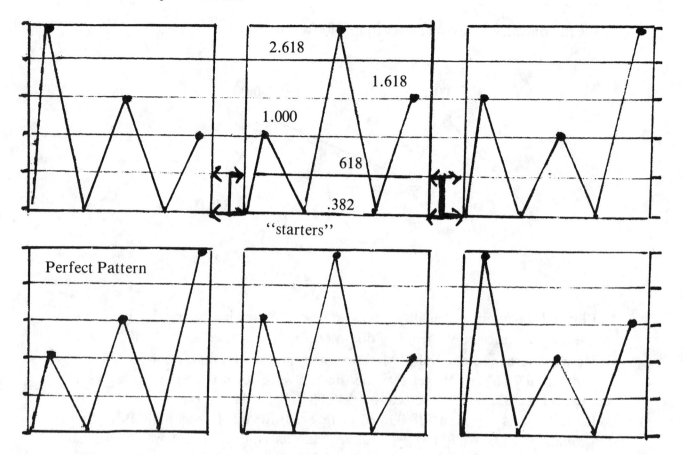

"starters"

Perfect Pattern

The actual price can be above or below the *peaks* of the six variations of the "Perfect Pattern Wave," but it won't be very far above or below.

Now, how do we know which "starter" value to use in advance? Well, in Part III of this book I have charted the complete 5-wave Intermediate patterns for each and every Bull and Bear Market over the *past 98 years*. Using this as a reference source (you won't find this in any other book) you *can* get the smallest wave value of *The Last Bull Market* before the present Bull move or the smallest wave value for *The Last Bear Market* before the present Bear move.

This will give you the "starter" value for Intermediate Waves (for example $38.00). Then use the next smaller Dollar value ($24.00) for your Minor wave "starter." If you find that you might need to adjust to the next smaller "starter" ($15.00) then by all means do so, but in most cases this won't be necessary.

If this ever happens to be the case though, you may want to keep track of all 3 Logarithmic Price Spirals, as the Intermediate Spiral does *confirm* the wave count of the Minor Spirals.

Our first example for this book will be the Bull Market that began August 12, 1982 and ended on January 6, 1984. For this market we will be constructing *two* charts:

Chart #1—for the Minor Waves. Its Dollar value "starter" will be for moves of $38.00 or more.

Chart #2—for Intermediate Waves. Its Dollar value "starter" will be for moves of $62.00 or more.

*Note:*   Bear markets will be detailed later on in Part II.

These "starter" dollar values will build two Logarithmic Price Spirals, one for Minor Waves and one for Intermediate Waves. The only difference is that they will be in chart form.

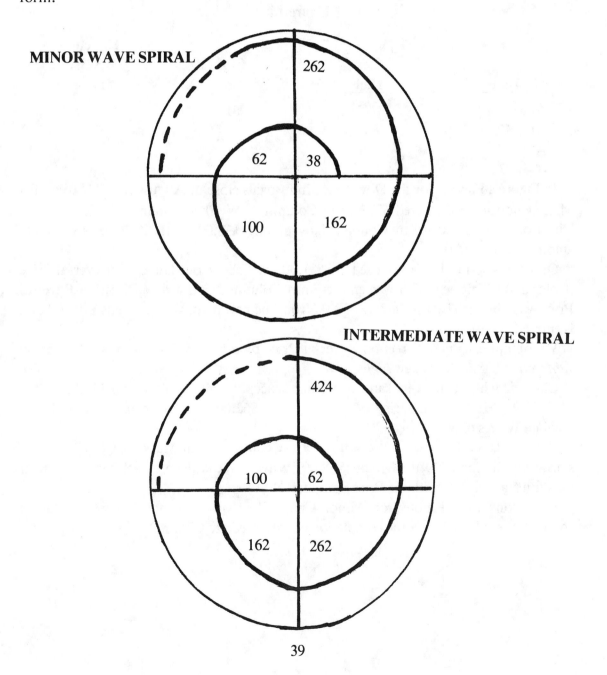

Start with Chart #1 for Minor Waves. With moves of $38.00 or more either up or down, we will be using the closing price on the Dow Jones Industrials each day.

In Column 1 we enter the dates.
In Column 2 we enter the close *if* it is a new *high*.
In Column 3 we enter the close *if* it is a new *low*.
In Column 4 we enter the *Direction Reversal Price*.

**Figure 15**

| Date | Close High | Close Low | Direction Reversal Price |
|---|---|---|---|
| Aug. 12 1982 | 777 | 815 | |
| Aug. 17 | 831 | | 793 |
| Aug. 23 | 891 | | 853 |

In Figure 15 above for the Dow Jones Industrials close of August 12, 1982 (the Bear Market bottom) we entered $777.00 in Column 3. We then obtained the level of the Direction Reversal Price in Column 4 by adding $38.00 to the $777.00 low close, amounting to $815.00.

On August 17th, the Dow closed at $831.00, well above our Direction Reversal Price (Column 4). This new high was entered into Column 2 and a new Direction Reversal Price was obtained by *subtracting* $38.00 from the new high, which equals $793.00 and is entered in Column 4.

We obtain each new Direction Reversal Price by *adding* $38.00 to new *lows,* or by *subtracting* $38.00 from new *highs.*

Chart #2 will use this very same procedure, except it will use a "starter" dollar value of $62.00 (.618), thus ignoring *all* moves under $62.00 and giving us the Five Intermediate Waves only.

Now, "Let's get started!" We will cover the complete Bull Market of 1982 to 1984, starting with Chart #1, the Minor ($38.00) Waves. We will note each wave count in Column 5 as our Logarithmic Price Spiral unfolds.

Extensions will be noted on Minor Chart #1. How to handle them in detail is completely explained after the completion of Intermediate Chart #2.

**Chart #1**
**MINOR WAVES...$38.00**
**Bull market Aug. 12, 1982 to Jan. 6, 1984**

| Date | Close New High | Close New Low | Direction Reversal Price | Minor Wave Count | Intermediate Wave Count |
|---|---|---|---|---|---|
| **1982** | | | | | |
| Aug. 12 | | $ 777. | $ 815. | | Dow Low |
| Aug. 17 | $ 831. | | 793. | | |
| Aug. 23 | 891. | | 853. | | |
| Aug. 26 | 892. | | 854. | | |
| Aug. 31 | 901. | | 863. | | |
| Sept. 9 | 925. | | 887. | | |
| Sept. 15 | 930. | | 892. | | |
| Sept. 21 | 935. | | 897. | 1 | |
| Sept. 30 | | 896. | 934. | 2 | |
| Oct. 6 | 944. | | 906. | | |
| Oct. 7 | 966. | | 928. | | |
| Oct. 8 | 987. | | 949. | | |
| Oct. 11 | 1013. | | 975. | | |
| Oct. 13 | 1015. | | 977. | | |
| Oct. 18 | 1019. | | 981. | | |
| Oct. 20 | 1034. | | 996. | | |
| Oct. 21 | 1037. | | 999. | 3 | |
| Oct. 25 | | 995. | 1033. | | |
| Oct. 28 | | 991. | 1029. | 4 | |
| Nov. 3 | 1065. | | 1027. | 5 | 1 |
| Nov. 15 | | 1021. | 1059. | | |
| Nov. 16 | | 1008. | 1046. | | |
| Nov. 23 | | 991. | 1029. | A | |
| Nov. 30 | 1039. | | 1001. | | |
| Dec. 6 | 1056. | | 1018. | | |
| Dec. 7 | 1057. | | 1019. | B | |
| Dec. 12 | | 1018. | 1056. | | |
| Dec. 14 | | 1009. | 1047. | | |
| Dec. 15 | | 993. | 1031. | C | 2 |
| Dec. 23 | 1045. | | 1007. | | |
| Dec. 27 | 1071. | | 1033. | 1 | |

41

## Chart #1 (Cont'd)

| Date | Close New High | Close New Low | Direction Reversal Price | Minor Wave Count | Intermediate Wave Count |
|---|---|---|---|---|---|
| **1983** | | | | | |
| Jan. 3 | | $1027. | $1065. | 2 | |
| Jan. 6 | $1071. | | 1033. | | |
| Jan. 7 | 1076. | | 1038. | | |
| Jan. 10 | 1092. | | 1054. | 3 | |
| Jan. 21 | | 1052. | 1090. | | |
| Jan. 24 | | 1030. | 1068. | 4 | |
| Jan. 31 | 1076. | | 1038. | | |
| Feb. 4 | 1078. | | 1040. | | |
| Feb. 7 | 1087. | | 1049. | | |
| Feb. 14 | 1097. | | 1059. | | |
| Feb. 24 | 1122. | | 1084. | | |
| Mar. 1 | 1131. | | 1093. | | |
| Mar. 2 | 1135. | | 1097. | | |
| Mar. 3 | 1138. | | 1100. | | |
| Mar. 4 | 1141. | | 1103. | | |
| Mar. 7 | 1142. | | 1104. | | |
| Mar. 24 | 1146. | | 1108. | | |
| Apr. 13 | 1157. | | 1119. | | |
| Apr. 14 | 1165. | | 1127. | | |
| Apr. 15 | 1171. | | 1133. | | |
| Apr. 18 | 1183. | | 1145. | | |
| Apr. 20 | 1191. | | 1153. | | |
| Apr. 22 | 1196. | | 1158. | | |
| Apr. 26 | 1209. | | 1171. | | |
| Apr. 28 | 1220. | | 1182. | | |
| Apr. 29 | 1226. | | 1188. | | |
| May 6 | 1233. | | 1195. | 5 | |
| May 19 | | 1191. | 1229. | | |
| May 20 | | 1190. | 1228. | ext. 6 | Extension of wave 5, as waves 6, 7 and 8 did not amount to $62.00 or more to qualify |
| May 25 | 1229. | | 1191. | ext. 7 | |
| Jun. 8 | | 1186. | 1224. | ext. 8 | |
| Jun. 14 | 1227. | | 1189. | | as Intermediate wave. See Chart #2. |
| Jun. 15 | 1237. | | 1199. | | |
| Jun. 16 | 1248. | | 1210. | ext. 9 | 3 |

*Note:* A full discussion of the extension of wave 3, above, will follow Chart #2.

**Chart #1 (Cont'd)**

| Date | Close New High | Close New Low | Direction Reversal Price | Minor Wave Count | Intermediate Wave Count |
|------|------|------|------|------|------|
| Jun. 28 | | $1209. | $1247. | | |
| Jul. 8 | | 1207. | 1245. | | |
| Jul. 12 | | 1199. | 1237. | | |
| Jul. 13 | | 1198. | 1236. | | |
| July 15 | | 1192. | 1230. | | |
| Jul. 18 | | 1190. | 1228. | A | |
| Jul. 26 | $1244. | | 1206. | B | |
| Jul. 29 | | 1199. | 1237. | | |
| Aug. 1 | | 1194. | 1232. | | |
| Aug. 2 | | 1188. | 1226. | | |
| Aug. 4 | | 1183. | 1221. | | |
| Aug. 8 | | 1163. | 1201. | C | 4 |
| Aug. 31 | 1216. | | 1178. | | |
| Sept. 6 | 1233. | | 1201. | | |
| Sept. 7 | 1244. | | 1206. | | |
| Sept. 8 | 1246. | | 1208. | | |
| Sept. 10 | 1249. | | 1211. | | |
| Sept. 11 | 1258. | | 1220. | | |
| Sept. 26 | 1261. | | 1223. | | |
| Oct. 6 | 1269. | | 1231. | | |
| Oct. 10 | 1285. | | 1247. | 1 | |
| Oct. 19 | | 1247. | 1285. | | |
| Oct. 28 | | 1223. | 1261. | | |
| Nov. 4 | | 1218. | 1256. | | |
| Nov. 7 | | 1215. | 1253. | 2 | |
| Nov. 14 | 1254. | | 1216. | | |
| Nov. 22 | 1276. | | 1238. | | |
| Nov. 25 | 1277. | | 1239. | | |
| Nov. 29 | 1287. | | 1249. | 3 | |
| Dec. 14 | | 1247. | 1285. | | |
| Dec. 15 | | 1237. | 1275. | 4 | |
| **1984** | | | | | |
| Jan. 5 | 1282. | | 1244. | | |
| Jan. 6 | 1287. | | 1249. | 5 | 5 |

By the first of February the Dow had fallen to 1212, a loss of 75 points. This clearly shows that the Bull market had ended, and we were then into wave A of a Bear move.

What we have actually constructed with Chart #1 is a series of Three Logarithmic Spirals, as pictured below.

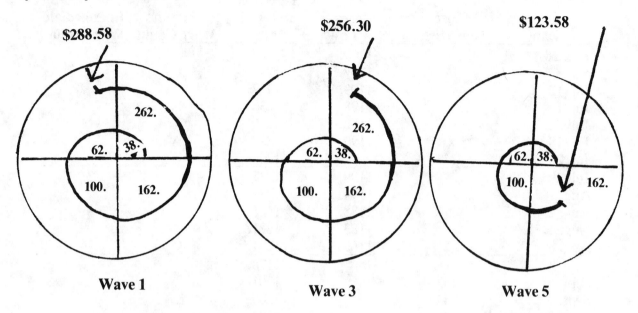

| Wave 1 | Wave 3 | Wave 5 |

### Chart #2
### INTERMEDIATE WAVES...$62.00
### Bull Market Aug. 12, 1982 to Jan. 6, 1984.

| Date | Close High | Close Low | Direction Reversal Price | | Intermediate Waves $62.00 Move |
|---|---|---|---|---|---|
| **1982** | | | | | |
| Aug. 12 | | 777. | 839. | Dow Low | |
| Aug. 20 | 869. | | 807. | | |
| Aug. 23 | 891. | | 829. | | |
| Aug. 26 | 892. | | 830. | | |
| Aug. 31 | 901. | | 839. | | |
| Sept. 3 | 925. | | 863. | | |
| Sept. 15 | 930. | | 868. | | |
| Sept. 21 | 935. | | 873. | | |
| Oct. 11 | 1013. | | 951. | | |
| Oct. 21 | 1037. | | 975. | | |
| Nov. 3 | 1065. | | 1003. | | 1 |
| Nov. 22 | | 1000. | 1062. | | |
| Nov. 23 | | 991. | 1053. | | 2 |

**Chart #2 (Cont'd)**

| Date | Close New High | Close New Low | Direction Reversal Price | Intermediate Waves $62.00 Move |
|---|---|---|---|---|
| Dec. 6 | 1056. | | 994. | |
| Dec. 7 | 1057. | | 995. | |
| Dec. 27 | 1071. | | 1009. | |
| **1983** | | | | |
| Jan. 10 | 1092. | | 1030. | |
| Feb. 14 | 1097. | | 1035. | |
| Feb. 24 | 1122. | | 1060. | |
| Mar. 4 | 1141. | | 1079. | |
| Apr. 18 | 1183. | | 1121. | |
| Apr. 20 | 1191. | | 1129. | |
| Apr. 22 | 1196. | | 1134. | |
| Apr. 26 | 1209. | | 1147. | |
| Apr. 29 | 1226. | | 1164. | |
| May 6 | 1233. | | 1171. | |
| Jun. 16 | 1248. | | 1186. | |
| Aug. 4 | | 1183. | 1245. | |
| Aug. 8 | | 1163. | 1225. | 4 |
| Sept. 6 | 1233. | | 1171. | |
| Sept. 8 | 1246. | | 1184. | |
| Sept. 22 | 1258. | | 1196. | |
| Sept. 26 | 1261. | | 1199. | |
| Oct. 10 | 1285. | | 1223. | |
| Nov. 29 | 1287. | | 1225. | |
| **1984** | | | | |
| Jan. 6 | 1287. | | 1225. | 5 |

Referring back to Chart #1, (page 41) and the extension that developed after Minor Wave 5 (Intermediate Wave 3)—How did we determine that Wave 6 was not the end of Wave 5, but part of an extension of Wave 5? By checking Chart #2 we could see that by June 14, Minor Wave extensions 6, 7 and 8 did not register a move of $62.00 or more down, and that Intermediate Wave 3 was *still* in progress.

The Minor Waves, as illustrated in the figure on the next page, that comprise Intermediate Wave 3 clearly show that the moves between May 6 and June 14 were not a legitimate part of corrective Waves A, B, C (Intermediate Wave 4). Rather, they were *subnormal* moves, or "retracements," developing into extensions 6, 7, 8, 9 of Intermediate Wave 3. The second figure on the next page shows how this wave *would have* looked *if* the extension had not developed.

45

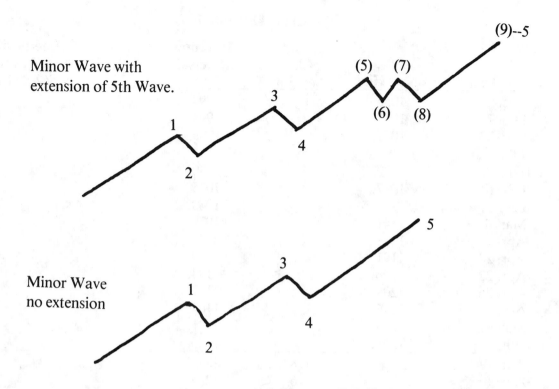

Minor Wave with
extension of 5th Wave.

Minor Wave
no extension

As was discussed earlier in Part I (the Foundation Basics of this book), if the shock value is exceptionally strong to Wave 5, 6, 7, 8, and 9 Wave extension of this wave will develop before the A, B, C correction will occur. The "clue" is the *6th* Wave, as it will be of a sub-standard strength. The 6th Wave here from the May 6 high of $1233.00 to May 20 low of $1190.00 had a total loss of $43.00. The *actual* A Wave that occurred later from the June 16 high of $1248 to the July 18 low of $1190 (resulting in a total loss of $58.00) showed the strength of a normal A corrective type wave.

Extensions can and do develop at times in Waves 1, 3 and 5 of any thrust move. We have to learn to "spot" them. Fortunately, with this Price Spiral Method we have Chart #2 to act as *confirmation* of a move.

Before going on to a discussion of the Bear Market, we shall take one last look at all the Intermediate waves in the Bull Market, for each has a "personality" of its own. Knowing what to look for and expect can be of great help to us as we "track" each wave along.

Wave 1—Starting from the low of the previous Bear Market, it almost always starts out quite slowly, and steadily gains buying momentum as it progresses to the point where it seems to temporarily slow down.

46

Wave 2—Some signs of selling, though not on heavy volume. I find that the point loss on this wave will be less than we can expect for wave 4.

Wave 3—Most of the time this is our "look out" for the extension wave. It is also the place we can expect to see the heaviest volume and can cover the longest time period.

Wave 4—The selling will be more active here than in wave 2, so a bit larger price drop can be anticipated in this wave.

Wave 5—Look for a gradual slowing of buying pressure and a slow increase of selling pressure. The point of balance between the two is near, and will signal the completion of this Bull Market.

## BEAR MARKETS

Bear Markets are the most difficult of all to track, as they have three different looks to the total move. So we are going to first become fully familiar with the three types we will encounter in our work.

All three types have normal downward thrust waves. The A Wave and the *Final* wave down, are each capable of developing extensions within them. However, it's the B (or B, C, and D) Wave that is so hard to define.

It was Elliott's concept that all Bear markets consisted of the type 1 (figure below) wave pattern for the Intermediate Waves, a simple 3-Wave move. Unfortunately, it is quite rare that the Bear Market ever assumes this simple look. In fact, it has only done so three times since 1897.

Instead, we almost always see a five wave pattern develop, as a check of the charts of the past markets from 1897 to the present, in the third section of this book, will show.

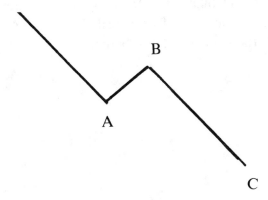

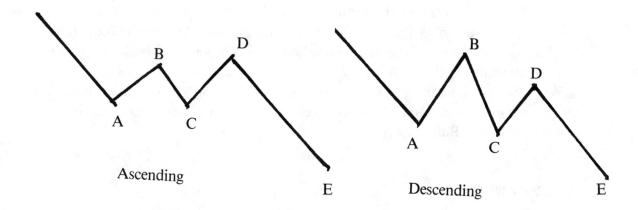

Ascending

Descending

Therefore, we shall most probably be working with a Five Intermediate Wave pattern, such as shown in the figures above. To further complicate our efforts, our Minor count for the B, C, and D waves tends to be quite irregular, sometimes only showing 1 or 2 Minor Waves in the total move. *It is more important* to keep very close watch on Chart #2, the Intermediate Wave count, during the development of the Minor Waves B, C, and D. *Only* Chart #2 gives us accurate *confirmation* of exactly where we are.

Elliott had his greatest difficulty with Bear Market patterns. The Price Spiral Method will eliminate this difficulty for us.

Since Bear Markets are of a smaller magnitude than Bull Markets, we will use the next smaller Dollar Value ratio (.236) or $24.00 for Chart #1, Minor Waves, but we will use the same $62.00 (.618) Dollar Value for Chart #2, the Intermediate Waves.

Our Bear Market example will be from April 27, 1981 to August 12, 1982. Our charts will be kept in exactly the same manner as before.

## Chart #1
## BEAR MARKET—MINOR WAVES

| Date | Close New High | Close New Low | Direction Reversal Price | $24.00 Moves | Intermediate |
|------|---------------|---------------|-------------------------|--------------|--------------|
| **1981** | | | | | |
| Apr. 27 | 1024. | | 1000. | | Dow Top |
| Apr. 30 | | 998. | 1022. | | |
| May 5 | | 972. | 995. | | |
| May 11 | | 963. | 986. | 1 | |
| May 15 | 986. | | 963. | | |
| May 28 | 994. | | 971. | | |
| Jun. 1 | 998. | | 975. | | |
| Jun. 11 | 1007. | | 984. | | |
| Jun. 15 | 1012. | | 988. | 2 | |
| Jun. 29 | | 985. | 1009. | | |
| Jul. 6 | | 949. | 973. | | |
| Jul. 14 | | 948. | 972. | | |
| Jul. 20 | | 941. | 965. | | |
| Jul. 22 | | 925. | 949. | 3 | |
| Jul. 31 | 952. | | 928. | | |
| Aug. 5 | 954. | | 930. | 4 | |
| Aug. 17 | | 927. | 951. | | Normal Thrust Wave |
| Aug. 18 | | 924. | 948. | | |
| Aug. 24 | | 900. | 924. | | |
| Aug. 27 | | 889. | 913. | | |
| Aug. 31 | | 881. | 905. | | |
| Sep. 8 | | 851. | 875. | | |
| Sep. 18 | | 836. | 860. | | |
| Sep. 25 | | 824. | 849. | 5 | A |
| Sep. 30 | 850. | | 826. | | |
| Oct. 2 | 861. | | 837. | | |
| Oct. 8 | 878. | | 854. | a | |
| Oct. 14 | | 851. | 875. | | |
| Oct. 19 | | 847. | 871. | | |
| Oct. 23 | | 838. | 862. | | |
| Oct. 26 | | 831. | 855. | b | |
| Nov. 2 | 867. | | 843. | | |
| Nov. 3 | 869. | | 845. | Ext. c | Does Not |
| Nov. 16 | | 845. | 869. | | Amount to |
| Nov. 18 | | 844. | 870. | Ext. d | $62.00 Move |
| Nov. 25 | 878. | | 854. | | Check Chart #2 |
| Dec. 1 | 890. | | 866. | | |
| Dec. 4 | 893. | | 869. | Ext. e (c) | B |

49

## Chart #1 (Cont'd)

| Date | Close New High | Close New Low | Direction Reversal Price | $24.00 Moves | Intermediate |
|---|---|---|---|---|---|
| Dec. 16 | | 869. | 893. | | |
| Dec. 29 | | 868. | 892. | | |
| **1982** | | | | | |
| Jan. 6 | | 861. | 885. | | |
| Jan. 13 | | 839. | 863. | 1 | |
| Jan. 28 | 864. | | 840. | | |
| Jan. 29 | 871. | | 849. | 2 | |
| Feb. 3 | | 845. | 869. | | |
| Feb. 9 | | 831. | 855. | | |
| Feb. 17 | | 828. | 852. | | |
| Feb. 22 | | 811. | 835. | | Check |
| Mar. 4 | | 807. | 831. | | Chart #2 |
| Mar. 8 | | 795. | 819. | 3 | C |
| Mar. 22 | 820. | | 796. | | |
| Mar. 23 | 827. | | 803. | | |
| Apr. 2 | 839. | | 815. | | |
| Apr. 8 | 843. | | 819. | | |
| Apr. 19 | 846. | | 822. | | |
| Apr. 26 | 866. | | 842. | | Check Chart #2 |
| May 7 | 869. | | 845. | a | D |
| May 17 | | 845. | 869. | | |
| May 20 | | 832. | 856. | | |
| Jun. 1 | | 815. | 839. | | |
| Jun. 9 | | 796. | 820. | | |
| Jun. 18 | | 789. | 813. | 1 | |
| Jun. 23 | 813. | | 789. | | |
| Jul. 12 | 825. | | 801. | | |
| Jul. 16 | 829. | | 805. | | |
| Jul. 20 | 833. | | 809. | 2 | |
| Jul. 30 | | 809. | 833. | | Abnormal |
| Aug. 4 | | 803. | 827. | | Thrust Wave |
| Aug. 6 | | 784. | 808. | | Check Chart #2 |
| Aug. 11 | | 777. | 801. | | |
| Aug. 12 | | 777. | 801. | 3 | E |
| | | | | | Bear-Bottom |

## Chart #2
## BEAR MARKET—INTERMEDIATE WAVES—$62.00

| Date | Close New High | Close New Low | Direction Reversal Price | Intermediate Wave Count | |
|---|---|---|---|---|---|
| **1981** | | | | | |
| Apr 27 | 1024. | | 962. | Dow Top | |
| Jul 2 | | 959. | 1021. | | |
| Jul 6 | | 949. | 1011. | | |
| Jul 14 | | 948. | 1010. | | |
| Jul 20 | | 941. | 1003. | | |
| Jul 22 | | 925. | 987. | | |
| Aug 19 | | 924. | 986. | | |
| Aug 24 | | 900. | 962. | | |
| Aug 27 | | 889. | 951. | | |
| Aug 31 | | 881. | 943. | | |
| Sep 8 | | 851. | 913. | | |
| Sep 18 | | 836. | 898. | | |
| Sep 25 | | 824. | 886. | A | − $200.00 |
| Nov 27 | 886. | | 824. | | |
| Dec 1 | 890. | | 828. | | |
| Dec 4 | 893. | | 821. | B | |
| **1982** | | | | | |
| Feb 22 | | 811. | 873. | | |
| Mar 4 | | 807. | 869. | | |
| Mar 8 | | 795. | 857. | C | |
| Apr 23 | 862. | | 800. | | |
| Apr 26 | 866. | | 804. | | |
| May 7 | 869. | | 807. | D | |
| Aug 4 | | 803. | 865. | | |
| Aug 6 | | 784. | 846. | | |
| Aug 11 | | 777. | 839. | | |
| Aug 12 | | 777. | 839. | E | Bear Bottom |

51

*Part II—The Price Spiral Method*

By August 20 the Dow had risen to $869.00, verifying our wave count, and the fact that we were definitely *now* into the Bull Market.

Well there you have it, a complete system that requires little time to keep up-to-date, and accurately tells us exactly which wave we are currently in and what to expect next.

Now we've seen how this method works for us in this recent time period—but how about the past? Let's give it the "Ultimate Test" and use the *two* most difficult markets in history to track, the Great Bull Market rise from March 30, 1926 to September 3, 1929, and the powerful depression era Bear Market that followed it, ending July 8, 1932. Could we have been prepared, beforehand, for the *top* and the *bottom,* using the Price Spiral Method? Let's see.

At this time the Stock Exchange was operating on a five and one half day week. The extra ½ day on Saturday does make it a bit more difficult, since the close for that day is only representative of "half strength" momentum and can be deceptive.

Also we are dealing with a market which represents the 5th Primary Wave, of a 5th Cycle Wave, of a 5 Super Cycle Wave. Looking at the following graph of this Super Cycle, which is scaled to size by computer, we see that the market from its beginning (1897) had not shown much of a price rise to this point (1926). We can reasonably expect this final move to be a relatively strong move up.

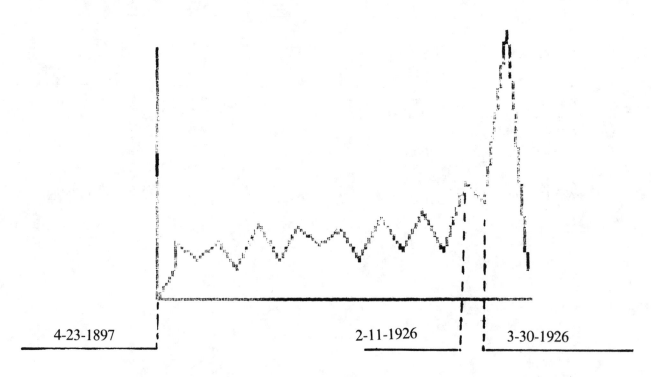

4-23-1897                    2-11-1926          3-30-1926

52

We also know that over a period of many years, as prices increase, so must we also increase our Dollar Value Ratios accordingly. However, it looks as if we probably would have been using the same Dollar Value Ratios now through quite a few of these past markets. We must be prepared to extend our range of ratios at any given time in this final Bull Move. Since we are expecting it to be a strong one, it follows that the Bear Market ending this 5th Super Cycle Wave will be quite strong and severe also, having to correct for the whole move-up since 1897. Our Dollar Value Ratios will also have to *decrease* faster than they had to with our usual *inner* Bear Markets.

As I said before, we are dealing with two of the hardest markets to correctly count, mainly because of their magnitude and velocity. They definitely are *not* the usual Bull and Bear moves that preceded them.

We now have an idea of what to expect and look for and know that we *must* be flexible and be prepared to increase and decrease our Dollar Value Ratios at a faster rate during these two Super moves.

We will start with a Dollar Value Ratio of .056, or $5.60, for the Minor Waves, and .146, or $14.60, for the Intermediate Waves. This is for the Bull Market.

*Note:* Because of the length of time these two markets span, each and every new close high, or close low was not listed. In many cases the close (high or low) at the end of the month was entered to keep the charts at a reasonable length.

## Chart #1
## BULL MARKET
## 3-30-1926 to 9-3-1929
## MINOR WAVES

| Date | Close New High | Close New Low | Direction Reversal Price | Minor Wave Count | Intermediate Wave |
|---|---|---|---|---|---|
| | | | Ratio | | |
| 3-30-1926 | | $135.20 | $140.80 | $5.60 | Dow Bottom |
| 4- 5-26 | $141.08 | | 135.48 | | |
| 4- 6-26 | 142.43 | | 136.83 | 1 | |
| 4-12-26 | | 136.53 | 142.13 | | |
| 4-14-26 | | 136.36 | 141.96 | | |
| 4-16-26 | | 136.27 | 141.87 | 2 | |
| 4-23-26 | 142.55 | | 136.95 | | |
| 4-24-26 | 144.83 | | 139.23 | 3 | |
| 5-10-26 | | 138.87 | 144.47 | | |
| 5-15-26 | | 138.02 | 143.62 | | |
| 5-17-26 | | 137.97 | 143.57 | | |
| 5-18-26 | | 137.53 | 143.13 | | |
| 5-19-26 | | 137.16 | 142.76 | 4 | |
| 5-28-26 | 143.43 | | 137.83 | | |
| 6-12-26 | 148.61 | | 143.01 | | |
| 7-17-26 | 158.81 | | 153.21 | | |
| 8-14-26 | 166.64 | | 161.04 | 5 | 1 |
| 8-25-26 | | 160.41 | 166.01 | a | |
| 9- 7-26 | 166.10 | | 160.50 | b | |
| 9-13-26 | | 158.97 | 164.57 | | |
| 9-30-26 | | 158.19 | 163.79 | | |
| 10-15-25 | | 147.95 | 153.55 | | |
| 10-19-26 | | 145.66 | 151.26 | c | 2 |
| 10-27-26 | 151.87 | | 142.87 | | At this point we shall raise our ratios to $9.00 (.090) for Minor Waves****** |
| 11- 9-26 | 154.82 | | 145.82 | | |
| 11-16-26 | 156.53 | | 147.53 | | |
| 11-26-26 | 157.37 | | 148.37 | | |
| 12- 4-26 | 159.05 | | 150.05 | | |
| 12-18-26 | 161.86 | | 152.86 | 1 | |
| 1-25-27 | | 152.73 | 161.73 | 2 | |
| 2-28-27 | 161.96 | | 152.96 | | |
| 4-22-27 | 167.36 | | 158.36 | | |
| 5-31-27 | 172.96 | | 163.96 | | |
| 7-30-27 | 182.61 | | 173.61 | | |
| 8-30-27 | 190.63 | | 181.63 | | |
| 9-15-27 | 198.97 | | 189.97 | | |
| 10- 3-27 | 199.78 | | 190.78 | 3 | |

54

## Chart #1 (Cont'd)
## 1929 BULL MARKET—MINOR WAVES

| Date | Close New High | Close New Low | Direction Reversal Price | Minor Wave Count | Intermediate Wave |
|---|---|---|---|---|---|
| 10- 8-27 | | $190.29 | $199.29 | | |
| 10-20-27 | | 183.00 | 192.00 | | |
| 10-22-27 | | 179.78 | 188.78 | 4 | |
| 11- 7-27 | $190.57 | | 181.57 | | |
| 11-29-27 | 198.21 | | 189.21 | | |
| 12-31-27 | 202.40 | | 193.40 | | |
| 1- 3-1928 | 203.35 | | 194.35 | 5 | |
| 2-17-28 | | 192.48 | 201.48 | | Insufficient correction for a Wave 6. See Intermediate Chart |
| 2-18-28 | | 191.80 | 200.80 | | |
| 2-20-28 | | 191.33 | 200.33 | ext. 6 | |
| 3-30-28 | 214.45 | | 205.45 | | |
| 4-13-28 | 216.93 | | 207.93 | | |
| 5-14-28 | 220.88 | | 211.88 | | |
| 6- 2-28 | 220.96 | | 211.96 | ext. 7 | |
| 6- 8-28 | | 211.51 | 220.51 | | |
| 6-12-28 | | 202.65 | 211.65 | | |
| 6-18-28 | | 201.96 | 210.96 | ext. 8 | |
| 7- 3-28 | 211.90 | | 202.90 | | |
| 7-30-28 | 216.62 | | 207.62 | | |
| 8-31-28 | 240.41 | | 231.41 | | |
| 10-29-28 | 257.13 | | 248.13 | | |
| 11-28-28 | 295.62 | | 286.62 | ext. 9 | 3 |
| 12- 6-28 | | 279.79 | 288.79 | | See Intermediate |
| 12- 7-28 | | 271.05 | 280.05 | | 4 |
| 12- 8-28 | | 257.33 | 266.33 | a | |
| 12-31-28 | 300.00 | | 285.40 | | We shall again raise our ratio to $14.60 (.146) for our Minor Waves |
| 1-31-1929 | 317.51 | | 302.91 | | |
| 2- 5-29 | 322.06 | | 308.00 | 1 | |
| 2-14-29 | | 306.49 | 321.09 | | |
| 2-16-29 | | 295.85 | 310.45 | 2 | |
| 2-25-29 | 311.24 | | 296.64 | | |
| 2-28-29 | 317.41 | | 302.81 | | |
| 3- 1-29 | 321.18 | | 306.58 | 3 | |

## Chart #1 (Cont'd)
## 1929 Bull Market—Minor Waves

| Date | Close New High | Close New Low | Direction Reversal Price | Minor Wave Count | Intermediate Wave |
|------|------|------|------|------|------|
| 3-11-29 | | 305.75 | 320.35 | | |
| 3-26-29 | | 296.51 | 311.11 | 4 | |
| 4-18-29 | 311.87 | | 297.27 | | |
| 4-30-29 | 319.29 | | 304.69 | | |
| 5- 4-29 | 327.08 | | 312.48 | 5 | |
| 5-22-29 | | 300.83 | 315.43 | | |
| 5-27-29 | | 293.42 | 308.02 | ext. 6 | See Intermediate Wave |
| 6- 4-29 | 310.57 | | 295.97 | | |
| 6-29-29 | 333.79 | | 319.19 | | |
| 7-31-29 | 347.70 | | 333.10 | | |
| 8- 3-29 | 355.62 | | 341.02 | ext. 7 | |
| 8- 9-29 | | 337.99 | 352.59 | ext. 8 | |
| 8-13-29 | 354.03 | | 339.43 | | |
| 8-30-29 | 380.33 | | 365.73 | | |
| 9- 3-1929 | 381.17 | | 366.57 | ext. 9 | 5 |
| | | | | | Dow Top |
| 9-12-29 | | 366.35 | | | |

## Chart #2
## 3-30-26 to 9-3-29
## Intermediate Waves

| Date | Close New Highs | Close New Lows | Direction Reversal Price | Intermediate Wave Count |
|------|----------------|----------------|--------------------------|-------------------------|
| 3-30-1926 | | 135.20 | 149.80 | Dow low using a $14.60 Ratio Value |
| 6-16-26 | 151.31 | | 136.71 | |
| 6-21-26 | 154.03 | | 139.43 | |
| 7-17-26 | 158.81 | | 144.21 | |
| 7-29-26 | 160.58 | | 145.98 | |
| 8- 3-26 | 163.40 | | 158.80 | |
| 8- 7-26 | 165.21 | | 150.61 | |
| 8-14-26 | 166.84 | | 152.24 | 1 |
| 10- 9-26 | | 151.18 | 165.78 | |
| 10-15-26 | | 147.95 | 162.55 | |
| 10-19-26 | | 145.66 | 160.26 | 2 |
| 12-18-26 | 161.86 | | 138.86 | we shall raise our |
| 2-28-1927 | 161.96 | | 138.96 | Ratio Value here to |
| 4-22-27 | 167.36 | | 144.36 | $23.00 (.23) |
| 5-31-27 | 172.96 | | 149.96 | |
| 7-30-27 | 182.61 | | 159.61 | |
| 8-30-27 | 190.63 | | 167.63 | |
| 9-15-27 | 198.97 | | 175.97 | |
| 10- 3-27 | 199.78 | | 176.78 | |
| 12-31-27 | 202.40 | | 179.40 | |
| 1- 3-1928 | 203.35 | | 180.35 | |
| 3-30-28 | 214.45 | | 191.45 | |
| 4-13-28 | 216.93 | | 193.93 | |
| 5-14-28 | 220.88 | | 197.88 | |
| 6- 2-28 | 220.96 | | 197.96 | |
| 8-31-28 | 240.41 | | 217.41 | |
| 10-29-28 | 257.13 | | 234.13 | |
| 11-28-28 | 295.62 | | 272.62 | 3 |
| 12- 7-28 | | 271.05 | 294.05 | |
| 12- 8-28 | | 257.33 | 281.33 | 4 |
| 12-31-28 | 300.00 | | 262.00 | We again raise the |
| 1-31-1929 | 317.51 | | 297.51 | Ratio Value to (.38) |
| 2- 5-29 | 322.06 | | 284.06 | $38.00 |
| 5- 4-29 | 327.08 | | 289.08 | |
| 6-29-29 | 333.79 | | 295.79 | |
| 7-31-29 | 347.70 | | 309.70 | |
| 8- 3-29 | 355.62 | | 317.62 | |
| 8-30-29 | 380.33 | | 342.33 | |
| 9- 3-29 | 381.17 | | 343.17 | 5 |
| 10- 1-29 | | 342.57 | | |

57

# Chart #1
## Super Cycle Bear Market
## 9-3-1929 to 7-8-1932
## Minor Waves

| Date | Close New Highs | Close New Lows | Direction Reversal Price | Minor Wave Count | Intermediate Wave |
|---|---|---|---|---|---|
| 9- 3-1929 | 381.17 | | 357.17 | $24.00 ratio | Dow Top |
| 9-24-29 | | 352.61 | 376.61 | | |
| 9-30-29 | | 343.45 | 367.45 | | |
| 10- 4-29 | | 325.17 | 348.17 | 1 | |
| 10-10-29 | 352.86 | | 328.86 | 2 | |
| 10-19-29 | | 323.87 | 347.87 | | |
| 10-23-29 | | 305.85 | 329.85 | | |
| 10-24-29 | | 299.47 | 323.47 | | |
| 10-28-29 | | 260.64 | 284.64 | | |
| 10-29-29 | | 230.07 | 254.07 | 3 | |
| 10-30-29 | 258.47 | | 234.47 | | |
| 10-31-29 | 273.51 | | 249.51 | 4 | |
| 11- 6-29 | | 232.13 | 256.13 | | |
| 11-11-29 | | 220.39 | 244.39 | | |
| 11-13-29 | | 198.69 | 222.69 | 5 | 1 |
| 11-15-29 | 228.73 | | 204.73 | | |
| 11-21-29 | 248.49 | | 224.49 | | |
| 12 7-29 | 263.46 | | 239.46 | a | |
| 12-20-29 | | 230.89 | 254.89 | b | |
| 1-24-1930 | 256.31 | | 232.31 | | |
| 1-31-30 | 267.14 | | 243.14 | | |
| 2-13-30 | 272.27 | | 248.27 | | |
| 3-29-30 | 386.19 | | 262.19 | | |
| 4-17-30 | 294.07 | | 270.07 | c | 2 |
| 5- 2-30 | | 266.56 | 290.56 | | |
| 5- 3-30 | | 258.31 | 282.31 | | |
| 6-24-30 | | 211.84 | 235.84 | 1 | |
| 7-17-30 | 239.07 | | 215.07 | | |
| 7-28-30 | 240.81 | | 216.81 | | |
| 9-10-30 | 245.09 | | 221.09 | 2 | |
| 9-30-30 | | 204.90 | 228.90 | | |
| 10-31-30 | | 183.35 | 207.35 | | |
| 11-10-30 | | 171.60 | 195.60 | | |
| 12-16-30 | | 157.51 | 181.51 | 3 | |
| 2-11-1931 | 181.88 | | 157.88 | | |
| 2-24-31 | 194.36 | | 170.36 | 4 | |

## Chart #1 (Cont'd)
## Super Cycle Bear Market
## 9-3-1929 to 7-8-1932
## Minor Waves

| Date | Close New Highs | Close New Lows | Direction Reversal Price | Minor Wave Count | Intermediate Wave |
|------|-----------------|----------------|--------------------------|------------------|-------------------|
| 4- 2-31 | | 169.89 | 193.89 | | |
| 4-29-31 | | 143.61 | 167.61 | | |
| 5-29-31 | | 128.46 | 152.46 | | |
| 6- 2-31 | | 119.89 | 143.89 | 5 | 3 |
| 6-22-31 | 145.82 | | 121.82 | | See Intermediate |
| 6-27-31 | 157.93 | | 133.93 | a,b,c | Wave 4 |
| 9- 4-31 | | 132.62 | 156.62 | | |
| 9-30-31 | | 96.61 | 120.61 | | |
| 10- 5-31 | | 86.48 | 110.48 | 1 | |
| 11- 6-31 | 112.72 | | 88.72 | | |
| 11- 9-31 | 116.79 | | 92.79 | 2 | |
| 11-28-31 | | 90.02 | 104.62 | | -------------------------we will lower |
| 12-17-31 | | 73.79 | 88.39 | | our ratio here to |
| 1- 5-1932 | | 71.24 | 85.74 | 3 | $14.60 |
| 1-15-32 | 85.88 | | 71.28 | | |
| 2-19-32 | 85.98 | | 71.38 | | |
| 3- 8-32 | 88.78 | | 74.18 | 4 | |
| 3-31-32 | | 73.28 | 87.88 | | |
| 5-31-32 | | 44.74 | 59.34 | | |
| 6-30-32 | | 42.82 | 57.42 | | |
| 7- 8-32 | | 41.22 | 55.82 | 5 | 5 |
| 8- 3-32 | 58.22 | | | | |

## Chart #2
## Bear Market
## Intermediate Waves
## * Because this is a *Super Cycle* correction—ratio will start at $62.00

| Date | Close New Highs | Close New Lows | Direction Reversal Price | Intermediate Waves |
|---|---|---|---|---|
| 9- 3-1929 | 381.17 | | 319. | Dow Top |
| 10-23-29 | | 306. | 368. | |
| 10-24-29 | | 299. | 361. | |
| 10-28-29 | | 261. | 323. | |
| 10-29-29 | | 230. | 292. | |
| 11-11-29 | | 220. | 282. | |
| 11-13-29 | | 200. | 262. | 1 |
| 4-17-30 | 294. | | 232. | 2 |
| 10-31-30 | | 183. | 245. | |
| 11-10-30 | | 172. | 234. | |
| 12-16-30 | | 158. | 220. | due to excessive |
| 4-29-31 | | 144. | 206. | loss, adjust ratio |
| 5-29-31 | | 128. | 190. ---------- | to $38.00 (.382) |
| 6- 2-31 | | 120. | 158. | 3 |
| 6-27-31 | 158. | | 120. | 4 |
| 9-16-31 | | 119. | 157. | |
| 9-30-31 | | 97. | 135. | |
| 10- 5-31 | | 86. | 124. | |
| 12-17-31 | | 74. | 112. | |
| 1- 5-32 | | 71. | 109. | |
| 5-31-32 | | 45. | 83. | |
| 6-30-32 | | 43. | 81. | |
| 7- 8-32 | | 41. | 79. | 5 |
| 9- 7-32 | 80. | | | |

I'm now going to sum up all we have learned in a step-by-step trading procedure.

## Step 1.

Decide first on at least 3 stocks (or 3 commodities) you want to "track." We all have our favorite stock, but some stocks run slightly ahead of or behind other stocks. They reach tops or bottoms before the rest, giving us clues as to what is ahead. If you are not familiar with the various stocks from which to choose your 3 from, study the business section of any daily major city newspaper, or a copy of the Wall Street Journal. The listings appear under column headings such as this:

| 52 Weeks | | | | Yld | P-E | Sales | | | | Net |
|---|---|---|---|---|---|---|---|---|---|---|
| High | Low | Stock | Div. | % | Ratio | 100s | High | low | Close | Chg. |
| 54¾ | 21 | Grumm | 1.60 | 3.2 | 22 | 590 | 51 | 49⅞ | 50¼ | – ¼ |
| 23⅞ | 18½ | Grum | pf2.80 | 12. | .. | 8 | 23⅜ | 23⅛ | 23⅛ | – ¼ |
| 39 | 11½ | Guardl | .36 | .9 | 17 | 204 | u39⅛ | 38⅝ | 38⅝ | – ⅜ |
| 27 | 11½ | GlfWst | .75 | 2.9 | 13 | 4711 | 26 | 25⅛ | 26 | + ½ |
| 57¾ | 49¼ | GlfW | pf 5.75 | 10. | .. | 1 | 57¾ | 57¾ | 57¾ | ..... |
| 158½ | 68¾ | GlfW | pf 3.87 | 2.5 | .. | 2 | 155 | 155 | 155 | +1 |
| 64 | 28¾ | GlfW | pf 2.50 | 4.2 | .. | 14 | 60¼ | 60⅛ | 60⅛ | – ⅜ |
| 35¾ | 24¼ | GulfOil | 2.80 | 8.9 | 6 | 3439 | 31⅝ | 31⅛ | 31⅜ | – ¼ |

Look at the high and low for the past 52 weeks. This is in the first and second columns appearing to the left of the stock's name or listing symbol. These figures give a close idea of the price range of the stock. Next look at the current close column. This tells us if the stock is near a high, making a new high, or dropping off in price.

## Step 2.

Once you have picked your stocks, the most important part begins. If a person is to pick a winner at the horse races, he needs to study the racing form and learn the past history and track record of his horse. So, too, must we learn the past history and performance of our stocks. Without it, we cannot correctly choose the right *Price Ratios* to track our wave patterns. To accomplish this we must study the history of our stocks for 3 to 5 years. The main sources of data are charts and graphs for each stock. The company that I have used most successfully is:

Securities Research Company
208 Newbury Street
Boston, Massachusetts 02116

This company will send you a single copy of their publication, called "Cycli-Graphs," which contains graphs on over 1,105 leading stocks. The graphs show monthly prices and cover 12 years. The cost of a single issue is $19.00 for issues from 1971 to the present.

They also publish a second type of issue, which is a *must* to us. It's called "Security Charts," is published monthly and covers the *weekly* prices of the 1,105 stocks for the past 18 months. Its price is $10.00 for a single issue, 1966 through present.

For historical tables on commodities write to:

Commodity Perspective
30 S. Wacker Drive, Suite 1820
Chicago, Illinois 60606

## Step 3.

While we are waiting for our stock chart history to arrive, we *must* also start to record the stocks current daily price close from the newspapers.* Once we are ready to begin using the Price Spiral Method and have learned the *right* ratios to use, we can start our Minor and Intermediate charts for our stocks.

## Step 4.

At this point, we have received our charts and graphs, and have been recording the daily close on stocks, commodities or indexes of our choice. Now we are ready to start constructing our Price Spiral charts.

---

*Note:* Local public libraries have back issues of the Wall Street Journal on file and on micro-film.

Below is a weekly chart of Commodity Price Trends, which will serve as our first example:

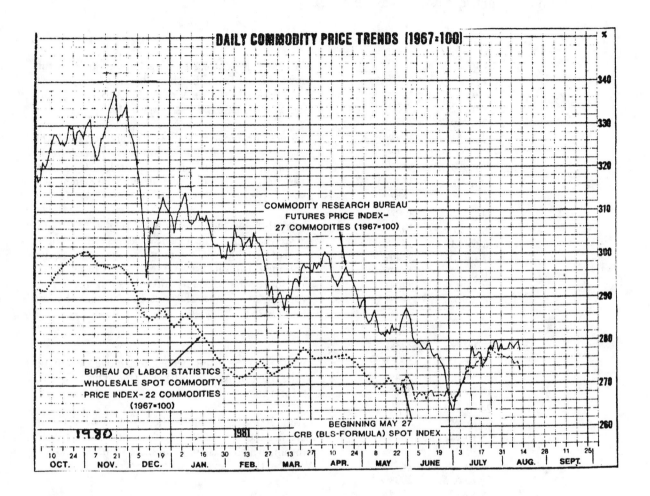

## Step 4. (Cont'd)

Looking at our example chart, we see the top of this bear move began in November, 1980...*This is our starting place.* We then go directly across to the scale on the right and find that the close for the week of November 14 to 21 was 338%. We mark this close down and continue on to the next week's close, again marking it down underneath the previous close.

63

*Part II—The Price Spiral Method*

This procedure is repeated for each week, until we have a complete listing for the entire move.

For our example the listing is as follows:

| | | |
|---|---|---|
| Nov. | 24 to 21 1980 | 338% |
| | 21 to 28 | 331% |
| | 28 to Dec. 5 | 334% |
| Dec. | 5 to 12 | 322% |
| | 12 to 19 | 295% A |
| | 19 to 23 | 310% |
| | 26 to 1/2/81 | 313% |
| Jan. | 2 to 9 | 305% |
| | 9 to 16 | 314% B |
| | 16 to 23 | 307% |
| | 23 to 30 | 300% |
| | 30 to 2/6 | 303% |
| Feb. | 6 to 13 | 306% |
| | 13 to 20 | 304% |
| | 20 to 27 | 294% |
| | 27 to 3/6 | 289% |
| Mar. | 6 to 13 | 288% C |
| | 13 to 20 | 294% |
| | 20 to 27 | 298% |
| | 27 to 4/3 | 298% |
| Apr. | 3 to 10 | 300% D |
| | 10 to 17 | 294% |
| | 17 to 24 | 297% |
| | 24 to 5/1 | 288% |
| May | 1 to 8 | 284% |
| | 8 to 15 | 281% |
| | 15 to 22 | 284% |
| | 22 to 29 | 287% |
| | 29 to 6/5 | 280% |
| Jun. | 5 to 12 | 278% |
| | 12 to 19 | 276% |
| | 19 to 26 | 268% |
| | 26 to 7/3 | 264% E |
| Jul. | 3 to 10 | 270% |
| | 10 to 17 | 278% |

Since we are isolating the *five* largest waves in this move, we see from the chart the first largest down move ended in the week of Dec. 12 to 19. This we label A. Calculate the loss at minus **43**.

The next up move was to 313%, and although the next week was a small down move, the *highest top* in this up move ended in the week of Jan. 9 to 16 at 314%. This we label B. We calculate the gain at plus **19**.

From 314% we move down our listing to 300%, and we see that for the next two weeks a small up move occurred to 306%. This move is too small, so we continue down our listing to Mar. 6 to 13 at 288%. We can see that by Mar. 20 to 27 an up move is in progress, so we label 288% as C. Calculate the loss at minus **26**.

From 288% the listing percentages move steadily up to the week of Apr. 3 to 10 at 300%. This is labeled D, for a gain of **12**.

From 300% we follow the listing down (again ignoring the smaller "wiggles") to the Bear move's bottom, which occurred Jun. 26 to Jul. 3 at 264%. We label this E, and calculate a loss of **36**.

THUS, WE HAVE ISOLATED THE FIVE LARGEST WAVES IN THIS BEAR MOVE!!!!

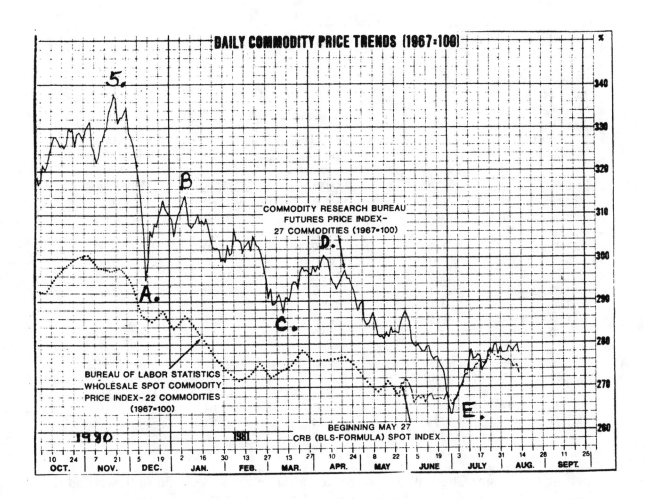

As you can see, it is a bear move, and I have labeled the 5 Intermediate waves A, B, C, D and E. They are clearly the *largest* moves in this downward move.

Now mark down the smallest amount gained or lost in these five waves...which in our example is **12** (wave D) and proceed to step 5.

## MASTER CHART
### For Locating Correct Fibonacci Ratio & Dollar Value

| Price Range of Lowest Reaction Wave **** 2 or 4 Bull Move B or D Bear Move From........To | Fibonacci Ratio | Converted Dollar Value For Intermediate Waves | Minor Waves | Alternate Minor Waves Next Lower Level |
|---|---|---|---|---|
| $62.00...$99.99 | .618 | $62.00 | $38.00 | $24.00 |
| 38.00... 61.99 | .382 | 38.00 | 24.00 | 14.00 |
| 24.00... 37.99 | .236 | 24.00 | 14.00 | 9.00 |
| 14.00... 23.99 | .145 | 14.00 | 9.00 | 5.00 |
| 9.00... 13.99 | .090 | 9.00 | 5.00 | 3.00 |
| 5.00... 8.99 | .055 | 5.00 | 3.00 | 2.00 |
| 3.00... 4.99 | .034 | 3.00 | 2.00 | 1.00 |
| 2.00... 2.99 | .0212 | 2.00 | 1.00 | .80 |
| 1.00... 1.99 | .0131 | 1.00 | .80 | .50 |
| .80... .99 | .0081 | .80 | .50 | .30 |
| .50... .79 | .0050 | .50 | .30 | .19 |
| .30... .49 | .0031 | .30 | .19 | .11 |
| .19... .29 | .0019 | .19 | .11 | .07 |
| .11... .18 | .0011 | .11 | .07 | .04 |
| .07... .10 | .0007 | .07 | .04 | .03 |
| .04... .06 | .0004 | .04 | .03 | .02 |

## Step 5.

Using the Master Chart above, we go down the left hand column until we find the range that the 12% from our example fits into. We see it in the 11¢ to 18¢ range. Going across the line for this range, we obtain the *dollar values* to use for our Intermediate and Minor Wave charts. We will begin constructing these in Step 6.

*This Master Chart will be used for each and every stock or commodity we track.*

## Step 6.

From the Master Chart we obtained the exact Fibonacci ratios, converted to *dollar values,* to use for our Intermediate and Minor Wave Charts. For our example they were:

> .11¢ for Intermediate Waves.
> .04¢ for Minor Waves (since this is a Bear move, and they tend to require the alternate ratios).

(We will not chart this last example at this point, as there are many other examples to follow later on in this section. Three different stocks will be analyzed in detail to best illustrate Step 6).

To refresh your memory, the chart composition for both the Intermediate and Minor Wave charts looks like this:

| Date | New Highs | New Lows | Direction Reversal Price | Minor Wave Count | Intermediate Wave # |
|------|-----------|----------|--------------------------|------------------|---------------------|
|      |           |          |                          |                  |                     |

We begin with the Minor Wave chart. Use the closing price of each of our 3 stocks each day. Keep 3 separate sets of charts, one for each stock.

In Column 1   We enter the date.

In Column 2   We enter the closing price *if* it's a New High, or if our Direction Reversal Price registers a direction change up.

In Column 3   We enter the closing price *if* it is a New Low or *if* our Dir/Rev price has signalled a direction change down.

In Column 4   We enter the Direction Reversal Price, which we compute each time we make a new entry in Columns 2 and 3. This Dir/Rev Price is obtained by *adding* our Dollar Value (Ratio) to *each* new Low entered, or by *subtracting* the Dollar Value Ratio from each new High entered.

In Column 5   We enter our Minor Wave counts, which are signalled by the Dir/Rev Price in Column 4.

The Intermediate Wave chart is handled in the same manner, only its Dollar Value is larger, and it registers only Intermediate Waves and ignores all Minor Waves. I would suggest you become *very* familiar with the chart keeping system by careful study of the examples in this book. *Practice eliminates error.*

One final word—*unless* an amount registers on your Intermediate charts, the Minor Wave trend is *still* intact, and will continue (expect extensions to develop) on *until* an amount does register on your Intermediate charts.

## THE PRICE SPIRAL METHOD APPLIED TO OPTIONS

The Price Spiral Method is especially effective and useful to the average investor, who does not have large amounts of cash to invest. Instead of buying stocks outright, this method can be used to purchase stock options.

For those not familiar with options, I will define them as the "renting" of stock shares for short periods of time, such as 3 months, 6 months and 9 months.

If you think a certain stock is going to rise, you can "rent" a block of stock on what is called a *call* option. If he thinks the stock is going to turn down, he "rents" the block on a *put* option, for one of the above amounts of time.

The "rent" he pays for the 100 shares is considerably smaller than what it would have cost him to buy 100 shares outright.

If the stock does indeed move in the direction he "bet" it would, then he stands to make a handsome profit. When he terminates his option, he receives the difference back between the price he paid for the option (based on what the stock was selling for at that time) and the price the option is worth when he sells it (based on the selling price of the stock at this new time).

Time can also erode the profit he stands to make. As the option gets nearer its expiration date, it begins to bring the profit down. So one would most surely wish to sell his option at the peak of its value, which is usually about 3 to 4 weeks before its expiration date.

Most Intermediate Waves run from 3 to 6 months in duration (Waves 1, 3, and 5) so you can see that the time length of options—3, 6 and 9 months—fit within the Intermediate Wave time lengths.

For example, if you bought a call option near the end of Minor Wave 5, Intermediate Wave E of a Bear Market, you would want to sell it ideally near the end of Minor Wave 5 (or ext. 9), Intermediate Wave 1 of this new Bull Market.

There is no system in existence that can tell you the *exact day* that a turn up or down is going to occur, for any stock or the Dow, but the Price Spiral Method will come very close.

In late July of 1982, using the Price Spiral Method, I suggested to a friend that he purchase a call option of 100 shares on a stock I had been tracking. The option would have cost him $38.50 (plus broker fees). He did not do so, but *if* he had he could have sold back his option 5 months later for a profit of $2100.00.

There are many good books on the subject of options, for those who care to learn more on them. I strongly urge anyone who is considering investing in options to learn all they can on them before they purchase them.

## Illustration of Trading Strategy For Maximum Profit

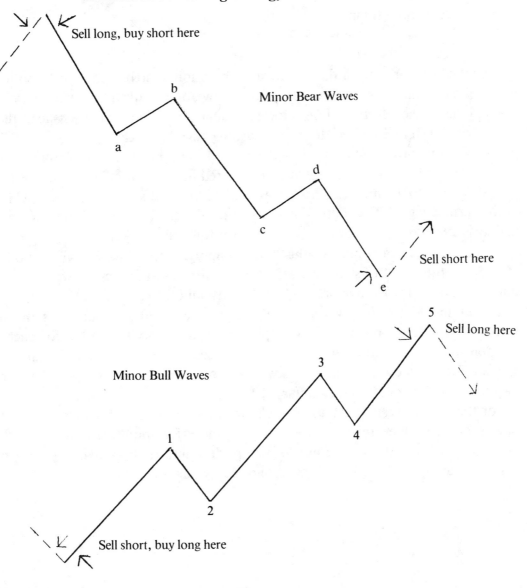

## UPDATING THE DOW CHART

For those wanting to update the Dow Jones Industrials Minor and Intermediate Wave charts for the current market in progress at the time of this writing (current Bear chart at end of this book) I suggest the following sources.

1.  The Wall Street Journal—the local library has daily back issues on microfilm.
2.  The Dow Jones Investor's Handbook—Published yearly, it contains a complete listing of the daily high, low, and close for all the Dow Averages and covers the past two years.

It can be purchased from local book dealers, or you can write to the following:

>   Dow Jones-Irwin
>   Homewood, Illinois 60430

Again, while you wait for the past data information to arrive, you must also begin to record the current daily closing price of the Dow Jones Industrials themselves. This is given in the business section of most local newspapers, and in the daily issue of the Wall Street Journal. It is also given during the evening news broadcast.

When this information is assembled, proceed to update the chart (on page 101) as outlined in the step-by-step procedure, as covered in Step 6 (and also discussed in part two of this book). Continue using the last Direction Reversal Price shown in Column 4 as the turning signal. Compute a new Direction Reversal Price each time a new entry update is made, using the same dollar values for this Bull Market.

While I have devoted most of this book to applying the Price Spiral Method to the Dow Jones Industrials, I shall now offer a few examples of the results we can obtain by applying it directly to individual stock and commodities.

The examples that follow will cover only the first and in some cases the second Intermediate Wave portions of the total Bull Market move of 1982 for each stock example presented. However, you can easily see the excellent performance of the system. Each of these example stocks went on to attain even greater price levels before the market topped out in early January, 1984.

For these examples, I have used stocks which I consider to be highly volatile. The first stock we shall examine is Teledyn. Using the Price Spiral Method, we shall chart the nine wave extensions of Minor Waves inside Intermediate Wave 1. Following is a graph of the 9 extension Minor Wave, followed by our system charts.

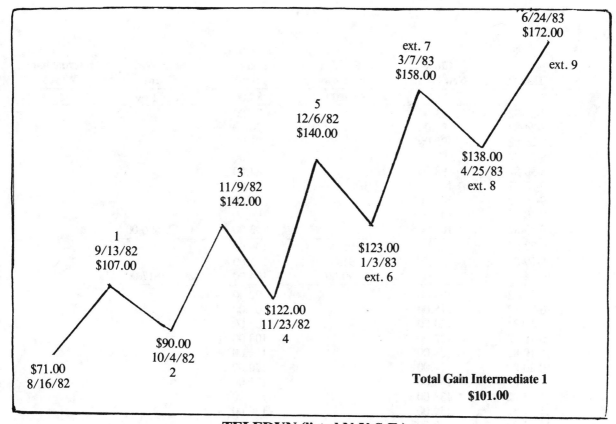

**TELEDYN (listed N.Y.S.E.)**

After studying past charts and price listings, Teledyn's Intermediate Wave price ranges were determined. using the Master chart, we determine the following dollar values:

.145 or $14.00 for Minor Waves
.236 or $24.00 for Intermediate Waves

This produced the following chart, calling each wave *exactly*.

## Teledyn

| Date | Close New Highs | Close New Lows | Direction Reversal Price | Minor Wave Count | | Intermediate Waves |
|---|---|---|---|---|---|---|
| 8-16-82 | | $ 71.00 | $ 85.00 | Stock Low | | |
| 8-23-82 | $ 85.00 | | 71.00 | | | |
| 8-24-82 | 88.00 | | 74.00 | | | |
| 8-25-82 | 95.00 | | 81.00 | | | |
| 8-26-82 | 97.00 | | 83.00 | | | |
| 8-30-82 | 98.00 | | 84.00 | | | |
| 9- 8-82 | 102.00 | | 88.00 | | | |
| 9- 9-82 | 103.00 | | 89.00 | | | |
| 9-10-82 | 104.00 | | 90.00 | | | |
| 9-13-82 | 107.00 | | 93.00 | 1 | + $36.00 | |
| 9-22-82 | | 92.00 | 106.00 | | | |
| 9-29-82 | | 91.00 | 105.00 | | | |
| 10- 4-82 | | 90.00 | 104.00 | 2 | − $17.00 | |
| 10-11-82 | 106.00 | | 92.00 | | | |
| 10-12-82 | 115.00 | | 101.00 | | | |
| 10-13-82 | 120.00 | | 106.00 | | | |
| 10-18-82 | 122.00 | | 108.00 | | | |
| 10-19-82 | 126.00 | | 112.00 | | | |
| 10-20-82 | 134.00 | | 120.00 | | | |
| 10-22-82 | 135.00 | | 121.00 | | | |
| 11- 3-82 | 138.00 | | 124.00 | | | |
| 11- 4-82 | 139.00 | | 125.00 | | | |
| 11- 5-82 | 141.00 | | 127.00 | | | |
| 11- 9-82 | 142.00 | | 128.00 | 3 | + $52.00 | |
| 11-22-82 | | 126.00 | 140.00 | | | |
| 11-23-82 | | 122.00 | 136.00 | 4 | − $20.00 | |
| 11-30-82 | 137.00 | | 123.00 | | | |
| 12- 6-82 | 140.00 | | 126.00 | 5 | + $18.00 | |
| 12-14-82 | | 126.00 | 140.00 | | | |
| 12-15-82 | | 125.00 | 139.00 | | | |
| 1- 3-83 | | 123.00 | 137.00 | ext.6 | − $17.00 | Wave 6 was clearly under the Intermediate Wave price ratio we set. This clearly shows an extension in progress through to Minor Wave 9. |
| 1-12-83 | 141.00 | | 127.00 | | | |
| 1-13-83 | 144.00 | | 130.00 | | | |
| 1-14-83 | 149.00 | | 135.00 | | | |
| 2-11-83 | 150.00 | | 136.00 | | | |
| 2-14-83 | 153.00 | | 139.00 | | | |
| 2-24-83 | 155.00 | | 141.00 | | | |
| 3- 1-83 | 156.00 | | 142.00 | | | |
| 3- 7-83 | 158.00 | | 144.00 | ext. 7 | + $35.00 | |

## Teledyn (Cont'd)

| Date | Close New Highs | Close New Lows | Direction Reversal Price | Minor Wave Count | Intermediate Waves |
|---|---|---|---|---|---|
| 4- 5-83 | | $144.00 | $158.00 | | |
| 4-19-83 | | 140.00 | 154.00 | | |
| 4-25-83 | | 138.00 | 152.00 | ext. 8 − $20.00 | |
| 5-25-83 | $152.00 | | 138.00 | | |
| 6- 1-83 | 153.00 | | 139.00 | | |
| 6- 2-83 | 155.00 | | 141.00 | | |
| 6- 6-83 | 156.00 | | 142.00 | | |
| 6- 7-83 | 159.00 | | 145.00 | | |
| 6- 8-83 | 162.00 | | 148.00 | | |
| 6- 9-83 | 167.00 | | 153.00 | | |
| 6-10-83 | 169.00 | | 155.00 | | |
| 6-24-83 | 172.00 | | 158.00 | ext. 9 + $34.00 | 1 + $101.00 |

Shortly after June 24, Teledyn lost well over $24.00 as it entered into Intermediate Wave 2.

An interesting "footnote" to conclude this example: During the Bull move in progress at the time of this writing, Teledyn reached a high (so far) of $302.00!

Our next example will be another highly volatile stock, Texas Instruments. We shall cover all the Minor Waves inside Intermediate Waves 1 and 2 with this example.

Texas Instruments began its bull move about two months before either the Dow Jones Industrials or Teledyn. This is a good reason to "track" more than one stock at a time. One can offer clues to what the other may do, as not all stocks run on the same time schedule.

I personally do not rate Texas Instruments as volatile as I would Teledyn. Therefore, I chose (again after *careful* study of its past price and wave movements) the Price Ratio of .090, or $9.00, for its Minor Waves, and .236, or $24.00, for its Intermediate Waves.

Here, too, Intermediate Wave 1 contained nine extended Minor Waves. Since this stock led the Dow and Teledyn, it gave a "clue" to watch for possible extensions in Intermediate Wave 1.

The following is the graph of all the Minor Waves as they occurred in Intermediate Waves 1 and 2, followed by the actual system chart.

## Texas Instruments

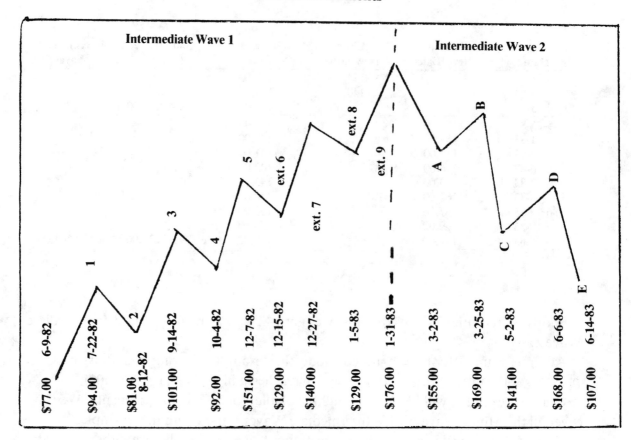

## Texas Instruments
## (listed N.Y.S.E.)

| Date | Close New Highs | Close New Lows | Direction Reversal Price | Minor Wave Count | Intermediate Waves |
|---|---|---|---|---|---|
| 6- 9-82 | | $ 77.00 | $ 86.00 | Stock Low | |
| 6-23-82 | $ 88.00 | | $ 79.00 | | |
| 7- 9-82 | 89.00 | | 80.00 | | |
| 7-12-82 | 90.00 | | 81.00 | | |
| 7-15-82 | 92.00 | | 83.00 | | |
| 7-20-82 | 93.00 | | 84.00 | | |
| 7-22-82 | 94.00 | | 85.00 | 1 + $17.00 | |
| 8- 4-82 | | 84.00 | 93.00 | | |
| 8- 5-82 | | 83.00 | 92.00 | | |
| 8- 6-82 | | 82.00 | 91.00 | | |
| 8-12-82 | | 81.00 | 90.00 | 2 − $13.00 | |

## Texas Instruments (Cont'd)

| Date | Close New Highs | Close New Lows | Direction Reversal Price | Minor Wave Count | Intermediate Waves |
|------|-----------------|----------------|--------------------------|------------------|--------------------|
| 8-23-82 | $ 90.00 | | $ 81.00 | | |
| 8-31-82 | 91.00 | | 82.00 | | |
| 9- 1-82 | 93.00 | | 84.00 | | |
| 9- 2-82 | 97.00 | | 88.00 | | |
| 9- 3-82 | 100.00 | | 91.00 | | |
| 9-14-82 | 101.00 | | 92.00 | 3  + $20.00 | |
| 10- 4-82 | | $ 92.00 | 101.00 | 4  − $ 9.00 | |
| 10- 8-82 | 102.00 | | 93.00 | | |
| 10-11-82 | 108.00 | | 99.00 | | |
| 10-12-82 | 109.00 | | 100.00 | | |
| 10-18-82 | 110.00 | | 101.00 | | |
| 10-20-82 | 114.00 | | 105.00 | | |
| 10-21-82 | 116.00 | | 107.00 | | |
| 10-22-82 | 118.00 | | 109.00 | | |
| 10-26-82 | 121.00 | | 112.00 | | |
| 11- 3-82 | 125.00 | | 116.00 | | |
| 11- 9-82 | 128.00 | | 119.00 | | |
| 11-10-82 | 129.00 | | 120.00 | | |
| 11-11-82 | 130.00 | | 121.00 | | |
| 11-12-82 | 132.00 | | 123.00 | | |
| 11-18-82 | 134.00 | | 125.00 | | |
| 11-30-82 | 136.00 | | 127.00 | | |
| 12- 1-82 | 137.00 | | 128.00 | | |
| 12- 2-82 | 139.00 | | 130.00 | | |
| 12- 3-82 | 140.00 | | 131.00 | | |
| 12- 6-82 | 147.00 | | 138.00 | | |
| 12- 7-82 | 151.00 | | 142.00 | 5  + $59.00 | |
| 12- 9-82 | | 140.00 | 149.00 | | |
| 12-12-82 | | 135.00 | 144.00 | | |
| 12-14-82 | | 131.00 | 140.00 | | Wave 6 was un- |
| 12-15-82 | | 129.00 | 138.00 | ext. 6 − $22.00 | der the $24.00 |
| 12-22-82 | 138.00 | | 129.00 | | Intermediate |
| 12-23-82 | 139.00 | | 130.00 | | Wave price ratio, |
| 12-27-82 | 140.00 | | 131.00 | ext. 7 + $11.00 | showing an ex- |
| 1- 3-83 | | 131.00 | 140.00 | | tension was in |
| 1- 5-83 | | 129.00 | 138.00 | ext. 8 − $11.00 | progress up to |
| 1-13-83 | 138.00 | | 129.00 | | ext. 9 Minor. |
| 1-14-83 | 148.00 | | 139.00 | | |
| 1-17-83 | 151.00 | | 142.00 | | |
| 1-18-83 | 155.00 | | 146.00 | | |
| 1-26-83 | 160.00 | | 151.00 | | |
| 1-27-83 | 161.00 | | 152.00 | | |
| 1-28-83 | 165.00 | | 156.00 | | |
| 1-31-83 | 176.00 | | 167.00 | ext. 9 + $47.00 | 1  + $99.00 |

75

## Texas Instruments (Cont'd)

| Date | Close New Highs | Close New Lows | Direction Reversal Price | Minor Wave Count | | Intermediate Waves | |
|------|-----------------|----------------|--------------------------|------------------|---|--------------------|---|
| 2- 2-83 | | $166.00 | $180.00 | because of the | | | |
| 2- 9-83 | | 162.00 | 176.00 | $99.00 price gain, | | | |
| 2-22-83 | | 161.00 | 175.00 | the ratio is raised | | | |
| 2-23-83 | | 159.00 | 173.00 | here to .145, | | | |
| 2-28-83 | | 156.00 | 170.00 | or $14.00 | | | |
| 3- 2-83 | | 155.00 | 169.00 | A | − $21.00 | | |
| 3-25-83 | $169.00 | | 155.00 | B | + $14.00 | | |
| 4-21-83 | | 149.00 | 163.00 | | | | |
| 4-22-83 | | 146.00 | 160.00 | | | | |
| 4-25-83 | | 145.00 | 159.00 | | | | |
| 4-29-83 | | 143.00 | 157.00 | | | | |
| 5- 2-83 | | 141.00 | 155.00 | C | − $28.00 | | |
| 5- 6-83 | 157.00 | | 143.00 | | | | |
| 5-24-83 | 158.00 | | 144.00 | | | | |
| 5-25-83 | 158.00 | | 144.00 | | | | |
| 6- 3-83 | 162.00 | | 148.00 | | | | |
| 6- 6-83 | 168.00 | | 154.00 | D | + $27.00 | | |
| 6-13-83 | | 118.00 | 132.00 | | | | |
| 6-14-83 | | 107.00 | 121.00 | E | − $61.00 | 2 | − $69.00 |

----note the Fibonacci Ratios
1.00 and .618 compare
to Intermediate Waves 1 and
2 in terms of price gain and loss.

Our next example is Digital Equipment. You will note that this stock's starting date is fairly well synchronized with the starting date of Teledyn and the Dow Jones on this Bull Move.

For Digital, I chose .090, or $9.00, for its Minor Waves, and .236, or $24.00, for its Intermediate Waves. Again, this was only after *careful* study of Digital's past price moves and using the Master Chart.

## Digital Equipment
## (listed N.Y.S.E.)

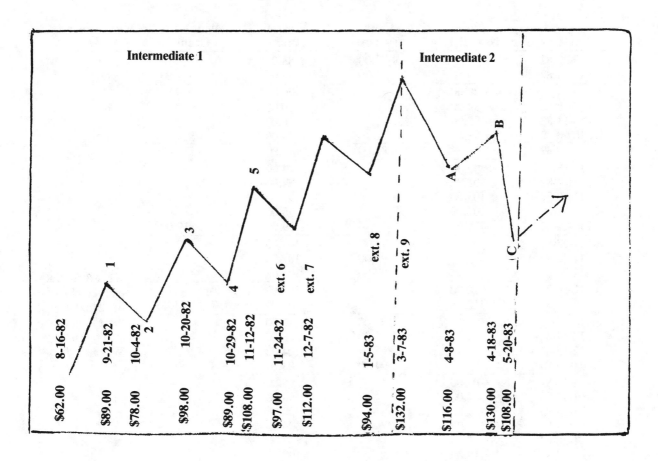

Intermediate 1    Intermediate 2

1    3    5    4    ext. 6    ext. 7    ext. 8    ext. 9    A    B    C

8-16-82    9-21-82    10-4-82    2    10-20-82    10-29-82    11-12-82    11-24-82    12-7-82    1-5-83    3-7-83    4-8-83    4-18-83    5-20-83

$62.00    $89.00    $78.00    $98.00    $89.00    $108.00    $97.00    $112.00    $94.00    $132.00    $116.00    $130.00    $108.00

## Digital Equipment

| Date | Close New Highs | Close New Lows | Direction Reversal Price | Minor Wave Count | | Intermediate Waves |
|---|---|---|---|---|---|---|
| 8-16-82 | | $ 62.00 | $ 71.00 | Stock Low | | |
| 8-20-82 | $ 71.00 | | 62.00 | | | |
| 8-23-82 | 75.00 | | 66.00 | | | |
| 8-25-82 | 78.00 | | 69.00 | | | |
| 8-26-82 | 80.00 | | 71.00 | | | |
| 8-30-82 | 81.00 | | 72.00 | | | |
| 8-31-82 | 84.00 | | 75.00 | | | |
| 9- 3-82 | 87.00 | | 78.00 | | | |
| 9-21-82 | 89.00 | | 80.00 | 1 | + $27.00 | |

## Digital Equipment (Cont'd)

| Date | Close New Highs | Close New Lows | Direction Reversal Price | Minor Wave Count | | Intermediate Waves |
|---|---|---|---|---|---|---|
| 9-30-82 | | $ 79.00 | $ 88.00 | | | |
| 10- 4-82 | | 78.00 | 87.00 | 2 | − $11.00 | |
| 10- 7-82 | $ 88.00 | | 79.00 | | | |
| 10- 8-82 | 89.00 | | 80.00 | | | |
| 10-11-82 | 95.00 | | 86.00 | | | |
| 10-20-82 | 98.00 | | 89.00 | 3 | + $20.00 | |
| 10-29-82 | | 89.00 | 98.00 | 4 | − $ 9.00 | |
| 11- 3-82 | 99.00 | | 90.00 | | | |
| 11- 4-82 | 101.00 | | 92.00 | | | |
| 11- 9-82 | 105.00 | | 96.00 | | | |
| 11-11-82 | 107.00 | | 98.00 | | | |
| 11-12-82 | 108.00 | | 99.00 | 5 | + $19.00 | |
| 11-22-82 | | 99.00 | 108.00 | | | |
| 11-23-82 | | 98.00 | 107.00 | | | |
| 11-24-82 | | 97.00 | 106.00 | ext. 6 | − $11.00 | |
| 12- 6-82 | 110.00 | | 101.00 | | | |
| 12- 7-82 | 112.00 | | 103.00 | ext. 7 | + $15.00 | |
| 12-13-82 | | 103.00 | 112.00 | | | |
| 12-14-82 | | 99.00 | 108.00 | | | |
| 12-15-82 | | 95.00 | 104.00 | | | |
| 1- 5-83 | | 94.00 | 103.00 | ext. 8 | − $18.00 | |
| 1-14-83 | 104.00 | | 95.00 | | | |
| 1-17-83 | 107.00 | | 98.00 | | | |
| 1-18-83 | 109.00 | | 100.00 | | | |
| 1-25-83 | 115.00 | | 106.00 | | | |
| 1-26-83 | 116.00 | | 107.00 | | | |
| 1-27-83 | 118.00 | | 109.00 | | | |
| 1-28-83 | 119.00 | | 110.00 | | | |
| 1-31-83 | 122.00 | | 113.00 | | | |
| 2-11-83 | 123.00 | | 114.00 | | | |
| 2-14-83 | 129.00 | | 120.00 | | | |
| 3- 7-83 | 132.00 | | 123.00 | ext. 9 | + $38.00 1 | + $70.00 |
| 4- 5-83 | | 121.00 | 130.00 | | | |
| 4- 7-83 | | 117.00 | 126.00 | | | |
| 4- 8-83 | | 116.00 | 125.00 | A | − $16.00 | |
| 4-15-83 | 128.00 | | 119.00 | | | |
| 4-18-83 | 130.00 | | 121.00 | B | + $14.00 | |
| 4-21-83 | | 121.00 | 130.00 | | | |
| 4-22-83 | | 120.00 | 129.00 | | | |
| 4-25-83 | | 118.00 | 127.00 | | | |
| 4-26-83 | | 116.00 | 125.00 | | | |
| 4-28-83 | | 115.00 | 124.00 | | | |
| 5- 2-83 | | 113.00 | 122.00 | | | |
| 5-19-83 | | 109.00 | 118.00 | | | |
| 5-20-83 | | 108.00 | 117.00 | C | − $22.00 2 | − $24.00 |

Wave 6 did not register a loss of $24.00, so there is an extension to Minor Wave 9.

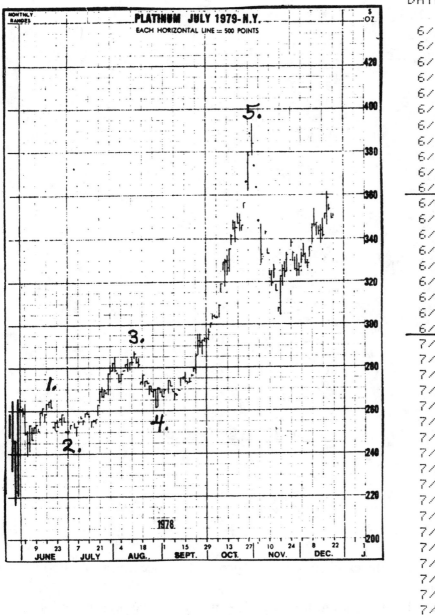

| DATE | PRICE | |
|---|---|---|
| 6/ 5/79 | 245 | |
| 6/ 6 | 253 | |
| 6/ 7 | 247 | |
| 6/ 8 | 252 | |
| 6/ 9 | 254 | |
| 6/12 | 251 | |
| 6/13 | 258 | |
| 6/14 | 262 | |
| 6/15 | 257 | |
| 6/16 | 263 | |
| 6/19 | 264 | 1a |
| 6/20 | 262 | |
| 6/21 | 253 | |
| 6/22 | 254 | |
| 6/23 | 253 | |
| 6/26 | 257 | |
| 6/27 | 258 | |
| 6/28 | 255 | |
| 6/29 | 250 | |
| 6/30 | 250 | 2a |
| 7/ 3 | 253 | |
| 7/ 5 | 252 | |
| 7/ 6 | 252 | |
| 7/ 7 | 255 | |
| 7/10 | 257 | |
| 7/11 | 256 | |
| 7/12 | 259 | |
| 7/13 | 259 | |
| 7/14 | 257 | |
| 7/17 | 255 | |
| 7/18 | 255 | |
| 7/19 | 256 | |
| 7/20 | 263 | |
| 7/21 | 269 | |
| 7/24 | 267 | |
| 7/25 | 269 | |
| 7/26 | 268 | |
| 7/27 | 277 | |
| 7/28 | 278 | |
| 7/31 | 282 | |
| 8/ 1 | 278 | |
| 8/ 2 | 277 | |
| 8/ 3 | 274 | |
| 8/4 | 277 | |
| 8/ 7 | 278 | |

| DATE | PRICE | DATE | PRICE |
|------|-------|------|-------|
| 8/ 8 | 282 | 9/22 | 285 |
| 8/ 9 | 280 | 9/25 | 293 |
| 8/10 | 283 | 9/26 | 292 |
| 8/11 | 283 | 9/27 | 293 |
| 8/14 | 286 **3** | 9/28 | 294 |
| 8/15 | 283 | 9/29 | 294 |
| 8/16 | 282 | 10/ 2 | 297 |
| 8/17 | 273 | 10/ 3 | 300 |
| 8/18 | 277 | 10/ 4 | 304 |
| 8/21 | 274 | 10/ 5 | 303 |
| 8/22 | 273 | 10/ 6 | 303 |
| 8/23 | 272 | 10/ 9 | 309 |
| 8/24 | 268 | 10/10 | 319 |
| 8/25 | 269 | 10/11 | 324 |
| 8/28 | 262 **4** | 10/12 | 324 |
| 8/29 | 271 | 10/16 | 326 |
| 8/30 | 268 | 10/17 | 335 |
| 8/31 | 266 | 10/18 | 342 |
| 9/ 1 | 269 | 10/19 | 348 |
| 9/ 5 | 274 | 10/20 | 345 |
| 9/ 6 | 272 | 10/23 | 348 |
| 9/ 7 | 269 | 10/24 | 346 |
| 9/ 8 | 267 | 10/25 | 357 |
| 9/11 | 269 | 10/26 | 366 |
| 9/12 | 275 | 10/27 | 378 |
| 9/13 | 275 | 10/30 | 388 **5** |
| 9/14 | 273 | 10/31 | 384 |
| 9/15 | 273 | 11/ 1 | 374 |
| 9/18 | 273 | 11/ 2 | 364 |
| 9/19 | 274 | 11/ 3 | 347 |
| 9/20 | 276 | 11/ 6 | 333 |
| 9/21 | 279 | | |

Our next example shows the excellent performance of the Price Spiral Method when applied to commodities.

From the above graph for Platinum for July 1979, we obtain the price close for each week (see listing on previous page and above).

After finding the price range losses and gains, and consulting the Master Chart, the following Dollar Values were applied:

.0007 or $ .07 for Intermediate Waves

.0004 or $.04 for Minor Waves.

This results in the chart shown on the next 2 pages.

80

## Minor and Intermediate Waves For Platinum (July 1979)

| Date | New Highs | New Lows | % Value $.04 Direction Reversal % | Minor Wave # | Intermediate Wave # |
|---|---|---|---|---|---|
| 6- 5-79 | | 245% | 249% | approx. bottom | |
| 6- 6-79 | 253% | | 249 | 1 | |
| 6- 7-79 | | 247 | 251 | 2 | |
| 6- 8-79 | 252 | | 248 | | |
| 6- 9-79 | 254 | | 250 | | |
| 6-13-79 | 258 | | 254 | | |
| 6-14-79 | 262 | | 258 | 3 | |
| 6-15-79 | | 257 | 261 | 4 | |
| 6-16-79 | 263 | | 259 | | |
| 6-19-79 | 264 | | 260 | 5 | 1 |
| 6-21-79 | | 253 | 257 | | |
| 6-23-79 | | 253 | 257 | a | |
| 6-26-79 | 257 | | 253 | | |
| 6-27-79 | 258 | | 254 | b | |
| 6-29-79 | | 250 | 254 | | |
| 6-30-79 | | 250 | 254 | c | 2 |
| 7- 7-79 | 255 | | 251 | | |
| 7-10-79 | 257 | | 253 | | |
| 7-12-79 | 259 | | 255 | | |
| 7-13-79 | 259 | | 255 | 1 | |
| 7-17-79 | | 255 | 259 | | |
| 7-18-79 | | 255 | 259 | 2 | |
| 7-20-79 | 263 | | 259 | | |
| 7-21-79 | 269 | | 265 | | |
| 7-27-79 | 277 | | 273 | | |
| 7-28-79 | 278 | | 274 | | |
| 7-31-79 | 282 | | 278 | 3 | |
| 8- 1-79 | | 278 | 282 | | |
| 8- 2-79 | | 277 | 281 | | |
| 8- 3-79 | | 274 | 278 | 4 | |
| 8- 7-79 | 278 | | 274 | | |
| 8- 8-79 | 282 | | 278 | | |
| 8-10-79 | 283 | | 279 | | |
| 8-14-79 | 286 | | 282 | 5 | 3 |
| 8-16-79 | | 282 | 286 | | |
| 8-17-79 | | 273 | 277 | a | |
| 8-18-79 | 277 | | 273 | b | |
| 8-22-79 | | 273 | 277 | | |
| 8-23-79 | | 272 | 276 | | |
| 8-24-79 | | 268 | 272 | | |
| 8-28-79 | | 262 | 266 | c | 4 |

81

## Minor and Intermediate Waves
## For Platinum (July 1979) (Cont'd)

| Date | New Highs | New Lows | % Value $.04 Direction Reversal % | Minor Wave # | Intermediate Wave # |
|------|-----------|----------|-----------------------------------|--------------|---------------------|
| 8-29-79 | 271% | | 267% | | |
| 9- 5-79 | 274 | | 270 | 3 | |
| 9- 7-79 | | 269% | 273 | | |
| 9- 8-79 | | 267 | 271 | 4 | |
| 9-12-79 | 275 | | 271 | | |
| 9-20-79 | 276 | | 272 | | |
| 9-21-79 | 279 | | 275 | | |
| 9-22-79 | 285 | | 281 | | |
| 9-25-79 | 293 | | 289 | | |
| 9-28-79 | 294 | | 290 | | |
| 10- 2-79 | 297 | | 293 | | |
| 10- 3-79 | 300 | | 296 | | |
| 10- 4-79 | 304 | | 300 | | |
| 10- 9-79 | 309 | | 305 | | |
| 10-10-79 | 319 | | 315 | | |
| 10-11-79 | 324 | | 320 | | |
| 10-16-79 | 326 | | 322 | | |
| 10-17-79 | 335 | | 331 | | |
| 10-18-79 | 342 | | 338 | | |
| 10-19-79 | 348 | | 344 | | |
| 10-25-79 | 357 | | 353 | | |
| 10-26-79 | 366 | | 362 | | |
| 10-30-79 | 388 | | 384 | 5 | 5 |
| 10-31-79 | | 384 | 388 | | |
| 11- 1-79 | | 374 | 378 | | |

*This clearly shows that the Price Spiral Method gives as excellent and reliable a performance on commodities as it does on stocks!*

(Copper prices had been in a Bear Market since Spring 1974)

## Intermediate Wave for Copper - May 1978 N.Y.
## With Five Minor Waves

| Date | New Highs ¢/lb. | New Lows ¢/lb. | Direction Reversal ¢/lb. | Level $ .04 Minor Wave Count | Level $ .07 Intermediate Count |
|---|---|---|---|---|---|
| 4- 1-77 | 76.5 | | 72.5 | | Approx. Top D |
| 4- 5-77 | | 72 | 76 | | |
| 4-15-77 | | 71 | 75 | | |
| 4-18-77 | | 68.5 | 72.5 | | |
| 4-26-77 | | 67.75 | 71.75 | a | |
| 5-14-77 | 71.75 | | 67.75 | b | |
| 5-20-77 | | 66 | 70 | | |
| 5-21-77 | | 65 | 69 | | |
| 5-23-77 | | 64.5 | 68.5 | | |
| 6- 5-77 | | 63 | 67 | | |
| 6- 7-77 | | 62 | 66 | c | |
| 6-17-77 | 68 | | 64 | | |
| 6-18-77 | 68.5 | | 64.5 | d | |
| 6-25-77 | | 63.5 | 67.5 | | |
| 7- 1-77 | | 61.5 | 65.5 | | |
| 7- 2-77 | | 60.5 | 64.5 | | |
| 7-26-77 | | 60 | 64 | | |
| 7-30-77 | | 58.625 | 62.625 | | |
| 7-31-77 | | 58.5 | 62.5 | | |
| 8- 6-77 | | 57.75 | 61.75 | | |
| 8- 8-77 | | 57.5 | 61.5 | | |
| 8- 9-77 | | 57 | 61 | | |
| 8-12-77 | | 56.25 | 60.25 | | |
| 8-13-77 | | 55.5 | 59.5 | e | E Bottom |

Copper prices advanced .904% to April of 1978 in a strong Intermediate Wave 1 of a Bull Move.

83

Again illustrating the value of the Price Spiral Method to the Commodity trader!

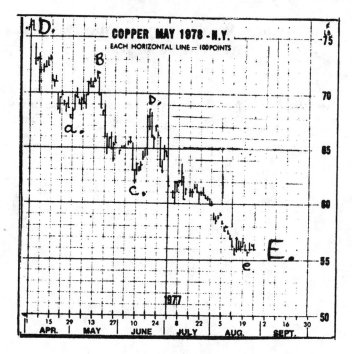

Here is an even more intricate commodity graph. Note how easily the Price Spiral System charts each and every wave with 100% accuracy.

After making a price listing and calculating the smallest reaction loss and gain, I obtained from the Master Chart the following Dollar Values:

     .0011 or $ .11  for Minor Waves

     .0031 or $ .30 for Intermediate Waves

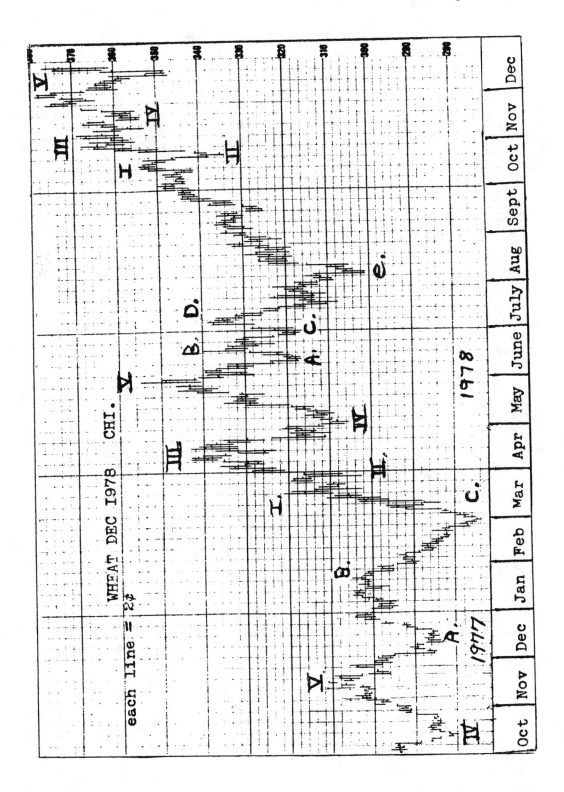

## Intermediate and Minor Waves
## For Wheat (Dec. 1978) CHI.

| Date | ¢/bu. New Highs | ¢/bu. New Lows | ¢/bu. Direction Reversal Level $ .11 | Minor Wave # Level $ .11 | Intermediate Wave # Level $ .30 |
|---|---|---|---|---|---|
| 11-16-77 | 311 | | 300 | 5 | 1 top |
| 11-22-77 | | 296 | 307 | | |
| 12-31-77 | | 285 | 296 | | |
| 12- 8-77 | | 283.25 | 294.25 | a | |
| 12-22-77 | 297 | | 286 | | |
| 12-26-77 | 300.75 | | 289.75 | | |
| 12-27-77 | 304.125 | | 293.125 | b | |
| 1-30-78 | | 291 | 302 | | |
| 1-31-78 | | 290.5 | 301.5 | | |
| 2- 7-78 | | 288.5 | 299.5 | | |
| 2- 8-78 | | 285.25 | 296.25 | | |
| 2-13-78 | | 284.5 | 295.5 | | |
| 2-15-78 | | 283 | 294 | | |
| 2-16-78 | | 281.5 | 292.5 | | |
| 2-24-78 | | 276.5 | 287.5 | | |
| 3- 1-78 | | 275 | 286 | c | 2 loss $ .36 |
| 3- 7-78 | 291.5 | | 280.5 | | |
| 3- 8-78 | 293.5 | | 282.5 | | |
| 3- 9-78 | 296 | | 285 | | |
| 3-14-78 | 301.25 | | 290.25 | | |
| 3-15-78 | 305.5 | | 294.5 | | |
| 3-16-78 | 305.75 | | 294.75 | | |
| 3-17-78 | 316 | | 305 | | |
| 3-28-78 | 319 | | 308 | 1 | |
| 3-30-78 | | 308 | 319 | 2 | |
| 4- 3-78 | 328.5 | | 317.5 | | |
| 4- 5-78 | 332.5 | | 321.5 | | |
| 4-10-78 | 335.25 | | 324.25 | | |
| 4-11-78 | 339 | | 328 | | |
| 4-12-78 | 341.5 | | 330.5 | 3 | |
| 4-24-78 | | 329.875 | 340.875 | | |
| 4-25-78 | | 311 | 322 | | |
| 5- 3-78 | | 310 | 321 | | |
| 5- 4-78 | | 308 | 319 | 4 | |
| 5-16-78 | 329 | | 318 | | |
| 5-18-78 | 330.875 | | 319.875 | | |
| 5-19-78 | 331 | | 320 | | |
| 5-24-78 | 341.5 | | 330.5 | | |
| 5-26-78 | 343 | | 332 | | |
| 5-30-78 | 349 | | 338 | 5 | 3 |

## Intermediate And Minor Waves
## For Wheat (Dec. 1978) CHI. (Cont'd)

| Date | ¢/bu. New Highs | ¢/bu. New Lows | ¢/bu. Direction Reversal Level $ .11 | Minor Wave # Level $ .11 | Intermediate Wave # Level $ .30 |
|---|---|---|---|---|---|
| 6- 2-78 | | 336 | 347 | | |
| 6- 5-78 | | 331 | 342 | | |
| 6- 9-78 | | 323.5 | 334.5 | | |
| 6-12-78 | | 318 | 329 | a | |
| 6-19-78 | 329 | | 318 | | |
| 6-20-78 | 334.5 | | 323.5 | b | |
| 6-28-78 | | 323 | 334 | | |
| 6-29-78 | | 318 | 329 | | |
| 6-30-78 | | 318 | 329 | c | |
| 7- 5-78 | 337.25 | | 326.25 | ext. d | |
| 7-12-78 | | 326 | 337 | | |
| 7-13-78 | | 322.75 | 333.75 | | |
| 7-14-78 | | 322 | 333 | | |
| 7-17-78 | | 317 | 328 | | |
| 7-18-78 | | 310.5 | 321.5 | | |
| 8- 7-78 | | 301.25 | 312.25 | ext. e | 4 |
| 8-14-78 | 315 | | 304 | | |
| 8-15-78 | 322 | | 311 | | |
| 8-16-78 | 326 | | 325 | | |
| 8-25-78 | 331 | | 320 | | |
| 9- 4-78 | 333.875 | | 322.875 | | |
| 9- 7-78 | 334 | | 323 | | |
| 9-20-78 | 337.25 | | 326.25 | | |
| 9-22-78 | 339 | | 328 | | |
| 9-25-78 | 340.875 | | 329.875 | | |
| 9-28-78 | 341.5 | | 330.5 | | |
| 9-29-78 | 341.75 | | 330.75 | | |
| 10- 3-78 | 349 | | 338 | | |
| 10-13-78 | 352.875 | | 341.875 | | |
| 10-16-78 | 353 | | 342 | 1 | |
| 10-23-78 | | 338 | 349 | | |
| 10-24-78 | | 335 | 346 | 2 | |
| 10-26-78 | 352.75 | | 341.75 | | |
| 10-27-78 | 359 | | 348 | | |
| 10-30-78 | 365 | | 354 | | |
| 11- 6-78 | 367 | | 356 | 3 | |
| 11- 9-78 | | 356 | 367 | | |
| 11-16-78 | | 354.5 | 343.5 | 4 | |
| 11-24-78 | 367.875 | | 356.875 | | |
| 11-27-78 | 375 | | 364 | | |
| 11-30-78 | 378 | | 367 | 5 | 5 |

The S&P 500 Index and the Dow Jones Industrials move together with suprisingly little disparity. This is clearly evident in the following chart of the monthly cash averages for both Indexes.

On major swings, they move pretty much together, although one or the other may boast that its index gave the first indication of such a move. On the whole, I believe the Dow Jones is apt to be more sensitive to short-term movements, and the 500-stock index provides a more reliable long-term perspective.

Following the monthly cash averages chart is a *complete* workup on the S&P 500. The complete record, from January, 1973 to June, 1987 is included. Look especially at the Bear Market beginning on January 6, 1981 and ending on August 9, 1982...and the following Bull Market starting August 9, 1982 and ending in January, 1984. We will use the Price Spiral Method to establish a past "track record," as a starting point for those interested in tracking the S&P.

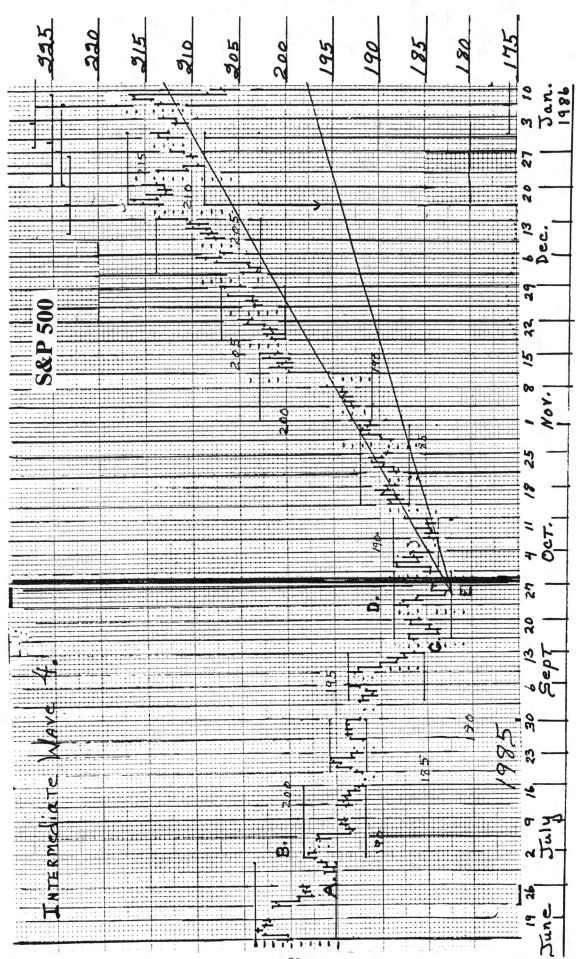

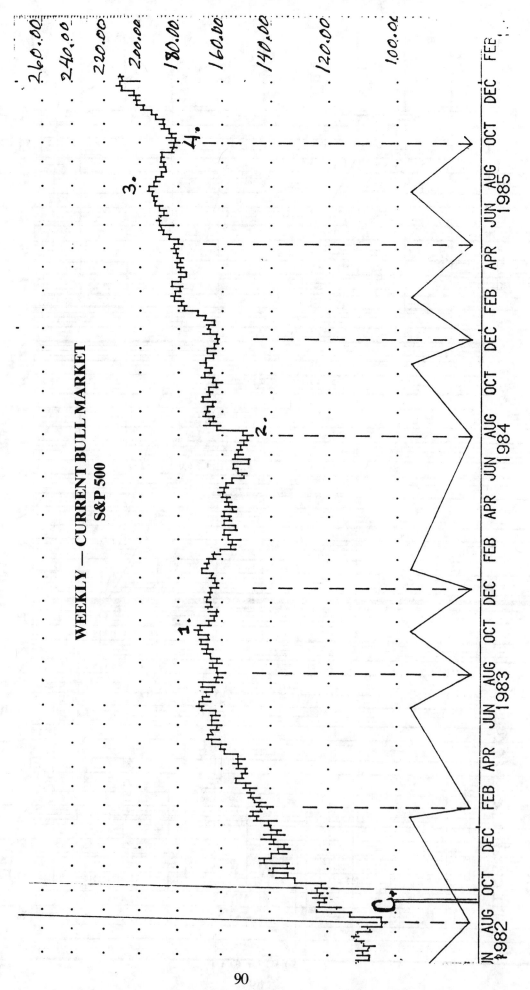

WEEKLY — CURRENT BULL MARKET
S&P 500

90

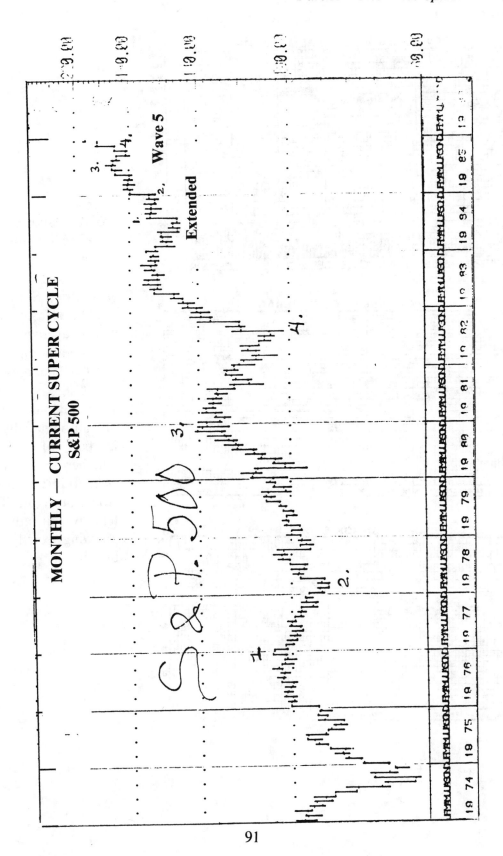

MONTHLY — CURRENT SUPER CYCLE
S&P 500

91

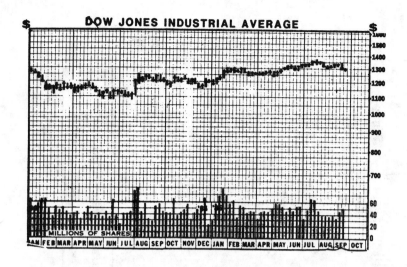

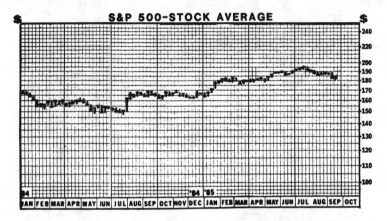

As you can see, all 3 averages are in phase with each other.

The Price Spiral Method can be effectively applied to any average, any stock, any commodity, with the same outstanding results.

It is obvious that profits are automatically a built-in part of this system, whether one buys options, commodities contracts, or stock outright. This system gives the advantage of knowing exactly *when* to buy or sell.

**S&P 500**
**Cycle Wave 4 — Bear Market**
**With Intermediate Waves Noted**

## Cycle Wave 4
## Bear Market With Intermediate Waves Noted
## S&P 500

| Mo. | Wk.# | Yr. | | | |
|---|---|---|---|---|---|
| 1 | 2 | 1973 | $119.25 | top | |
| 1 | 3 | | 119.00 | | |
| 1 | 4 | | 116.50 | | |
| 1 | 5 | | 114.25 | | |
| 2 | 1 | | 114.75 | | |
| 2 | 2 | | 115.00 | | |
| 2 | 3 | | 113.25 | | |
| 2 | 4 | | 112.50 | | |
| 3 | 1 | | 113.75 | | |
| 3 | 2 | | 113.50 | | |
| 3 | 3 | | 109.00 | | |
| 3 | 4 | | 109.75 | | |
| 4 | 1 | | 109.50 | | |
| 4 | 2 | | 112.00 | | |
| 4 | 3 | | 112.25 | | |
| 4 | 4 | | 107.25 | | |
| 5 | 1 | | 111.00 | | |
| 5 | 2 | | 108.25 | | |
| 5 | 3 | | 103.85* | | |
| 5 | 4 | | 108.00* | | |
| 5 | 5 | | 104.00 | | |
| 6 | 1 | | 107.00 | | |
| 6 | 2 | | 105.00 | | |
| 6 | 3 | | 103.75 | | |
| 6 | 4 | | 104.00 | | |
| 7 | 1 | | 102.25* | | |
| 7 | 2 | | 104.00 | | |
| 7 | 3 | | 107.00 | | |
| 7 | 4 | | 109.50* | | |
| 8 | 1 | | 106.75 | | |
| 8 | 2 | | 104.75 | | |
| 8 | 3 | | 102.50 | | -17.50 |
| 8 | 4 | | 101.75* | A | |

*********************************

| Mo. | Wk.# | Yr. | | | |
|---|---|---|---|---|---|
| 8 | 5 | | 104.25 | | |
| 9 | 1 | | 105.00 | | |
| 9 | 2 | | 104.50 | | |
| 9 | 3 | | 107.25 | | |
| 9 | 4 | | 108.50 | | |
| 10 | 1 | | 109.85 | | |
| 10 | 2 | | 111.25 | | +9.50 |
| 10 | 3 | | 110.15 | | |
| 10 | 4 | | 111.25* | B | |

*********************************

| Mo. | Wk.# | Yr. | | |
|---|---|---|---|---|
| 10 | 5 | | 107.00 | |
| 11 | 1 | | 105.25 | |
| 11 | 2 | | 104.00 | |
| 11 | 3 | | 99.50 | |

| Mo. | Wk.# | Yr. | | | |
|---|---|---|---|---|---|
| 11 | 4 | 1973 | $ 96.00 | | |
| 12 | 1 | | 96.75 | | |
| 12 | 2 | | 93.25* | C | -18.00 |
| 12 | 3 | | 94.75 | | |
| 12 | 4 | | 97.50 | | |
| 1 | 1 | 1974 | 98.75 | | |
| 1 | 2 | | 93.50 | | |
| 1 | 3 | | 95.50 | | |
| 1 | 4 | | 96.75 | | |
| 1 | 5 | | 95.25 | | |
| 2 | 1 | | 92.25 | | |
| 2 | 2 | | 92.25 | | |
| 2 | 3 | | 92.50 | | |
| 2 | 4 | | 95.25 | | |
| 3 | 1 | | 98.00 | | |
| 3 | 2 | | 99.25* | D | +6.00 |
| 3 | 3 | | 97.15 | | |
| 3 | 4 | | 94.00 | | |
| 4 | 1 | | 93.00 | | |
| 4 | 2 | | 92.25 | | |
| 4 | 3 | | 93.75 | | |
| 4 | 4 | | 90.25 | | |
| 5 | 1 | | 92.50 | | |
| 5 | 2 | | 91.50 | | |
| 5 | 3 | | 88.25 | | |
| 5 | 4 | | 88.75 | | |
| 5 | 5 | | 87.15 | | |
| 6 | 1 | | 92.75 | | |
| 6 | 2 | | 91.00 | | |
| 6 | 3 | | 87.25 | | |
| 6 | 4 | | 86.00 | | |
| 7 | 1 | | 83.50 | | |
| 7 | 2 | | 83.00 | | |
| 7 | 3 | | 83.25 | | |
| 7 | 4 | | 82.50 | | |
| 7 | 5 | | 78.75 | | |
| 8 | 1 | | 81.00 | | |
| 8 | 2 | | 75.75 | | |
| 8 | 3 | | 71.50 | | |
| 8 | 4 | | 72.15 | | |
| 9 | 1 | | 71.50 | | |
| 9 | 2 | | 65.25 | | |
| 9 | 3 | | 70.00 | | |
| 9 | 4 | | 65.00 | | |
| 10 | 1 | | 62.50* | E | -36.75 |

*********************************

**S & P 500**
**Cycle Wave 5**
**Primary Waves Included**

## Part II—The Price Spiral Method

## Cycle Wave 5—Bull Market
## Primary Wave 1
## With Intermediate Waves Noted
## S&P 500

| Mo. Wk.# Yr. | | Mo. Wk.# Yr. | | Mo. Wk.# Yr. | |
|---|---|---|---|---|---|
| 10- 2-1974 | $ 71.00 | 8- 1 | 86.00 | 6- 4 | 103.75 |
| 10- 3 | 72.50 | 8- 2 | 86.25 | 6- 5 | 104.00 |
| 10- 4 | 70.15 | 8- 3 | 84.50*4 | 7- 1 | 105.00 |
| 10- 5 | 73.95 | ********************** | | 7- 2 | 104.75 |
| 11- 1 | 75.00* 1 | 8- 4 | 87.00 | 7- 3 | 104.00 |
| ********************** | | 9- 1 | 85.50 | 7- 4 | 103.25 |
| 11- 2 | 71.85 | 9- 2 | 85.25 | 8- 1 | 103.75 |
| 11- 3 | 69.00 | 9- 3 | 86.00 | 8- 2 | 104.25 |
| 11- 4 | 69.85 | 9- 4 | 86.20 | 8- 3 | 102.5 |
| 12- 1 | 65.00* 2 | 10- 1 | 86.00 | 8- 4 | 101.50 |
| ********************** | | 10- 2 | 88.00 | 9- 1 | 104.25 |
| 12- 2 | 67.00 | 10- 3 | 89.00 | 9- 2 | 104.50 |
| 12- 3 | 66.85 | 10- 4 | 90.00 | 9- 3 | 106.25 |
| 12- 4 | 67.00 | 10- 5 | 89.20 | 9- 4 | 106.75 |
| 1- 1-1975 | 70.80 | 11- 1 | 89.75 | 9- 5 | 104.00 |
| 1- 2 | 72.75 | 11- 2 | 91.00 | 10- 1 | 102.50 |
| 1- 3 | 71.00 | 11- 3 | 89.90 | 10- 2 | 101.00 |
| 1- 4 | 73.00 | 11- 4 | 91.50 | 10- 3 | 100.00 |
| 1- 5 | 77.00 | 12- 1 | 86.75 | 10- 4 | 103.00 |
| 2- 1 | 78.50 | 12- 2 | 87.90 | 11- 1 | 101.00 |
| 2- 2 | 81.35 | 12- 3 | 89.00 | 11- 2 | 99.25 |
| 2- 3 | 82.50 | 12- 4 | 90.25 | 11- 3 | 101.90 |
| 2- 4 | 81.50 | 12- 5 | 91.00 | 11- 4 | 103.25 |
| 3- 1 | 84.50 | 1- 1-1976 | 95.00 | 12- 1 | 103.00 |
| 3- 2 | 85.00 | 1- 2 | 97.15 | 12- 2 | 104.75 |
| 3- 3 | 83.50 | 1- 3 | 99.25 | 12- 3 | 104.25 |
| 3- 4 | 83.85 | 1- 4 | 101.00 | 12- 4 | 105.00 |
| 4- 1 | 81.00 | 2- 1 | 99.87 | 12- 5 | 107.50* 5 |
| 4- 2 | 84.20 | 2- 2 | 99.90 | ********************** | |
| 4- 3 | 86.25 | 2- 3 | 102.10 | | |
| 4- 4 | 86.50 | 2- 4 | 100.00 | | |
| 4- 5 | 89.50 | 3- 1 | 99.20 | | |
| 5- 1 | 90.75 | 3- 2 | 101.00 | | |
| 5- 2 | 90.50 | 3- 3 | 100.00 | | |
| 5- 3 | 90.80 | 3- 4 | 102.80 | | |
| 5- 4 | 90.80 | 3- 5 | 102.20 | | |
| 6- 1 | 92.85 | 4- 1 | 100.50 | | |
| 6- 2 | 91.75 | 4- 2 | 101.00 | | |
| 6- 3 | 92.85 | 4- 3 | 102.35 | | |
| 6- 4 | 95.00* 3 | 4- 4 | 101.75 | | |
| ********************** | | 5- 1 | 102.00 | | |
| 7- 1 | 94.50 | 5- 2 | 102.50 | | |
| 7- 2 | 94.75 | 5- 3 | 102.00 | | |
| 7- 3 | 93.00 | 5- 4 | 100.00 | | |
| 7- 4 | 89.26 | 6- 1 | 99.10 | | |
| 7- 5 | 88.00 | 6- 2 | 101.00 | | |
| | | 6- 3 | 103.85 | | |

99

**Cycle Wave 5—Bear Market**
**Primary Wave 2**
**With Intermediate Waves Noted**
**S&P 500**

| Mo. Wk. # Yr. | | | Mo. Wk. # Yr. | | |
|---|---|---|---|---|---|
| 1- 1-1977 | $105.00 | | 10- 1 | 96.99 | |
| 1- 2 | 104.00 | | 10- 2 | 93.50 | |
| 1- 3 | 103.25 | | 10- 3 | 92.45 | |
| 1- 4 | 101.90 | | 10- 4 | 92.95 | |
| 2- 1 | 101.75 | | 11- 1 | 91.50 | *C |
| 2- 2 | 100.25 | | 11- 2 | 96.00 | |
| 2- 3 | 100.50 | | 11- 3 | 95.10 | |
| 2- 4 | 99.50 | | 11- 4 | 96.75 | *D |
| 3- 1 | 101.50 | | 11- 5 | 94.70 | |
| 3- 2 | 100.90 | | 12- 1 | 93.50 | |
| 3- 3 | 101.95 | | 12- 2 | 93.25 | |
| 3- 4 | 99.00 | | 12- 3 | 94.75 | |
| 3- 5 | 98.90 | | 12- 4 | 95.10 | |
| 4- 1 | 98.10 | | 1- 1-1978 | 91.75 | |
| 4- 2 | 102.20 | | 1- 2 | 89.90 | |
| 4- 3 | 98.85 | | 1- 3 | 89.80 | |
| 4- 4 | 98.80 | | 1- 4 | 88.85 | |
| 5- 1 | 99.50 | | 2- 1 | 89.90 | |
| 5- 2 | 99.10 | | 2- 2 | 90.00 | |
| 5- 3 | 99.50 | | 2- 3 | 88.00 | |
| 5- 4 | 96.00 | * A | 2- 4 | 88.65 | |
| 6- 1 | 97.75 | | 3- 1 | 87.40 | * E |
| 6- 2 | 98.50 | | | | |
| 6- 3 | 99.90 | | | | |
| 6- 4 | 101.25 | | | | |
| 6- 5 | 100.00 | | | | |
| 7- 1 | 99.75 | | | | |
| 7- 2 | 100.15 | | | | |
| 7- 3 | 101.50 | * B | | | |
| 7- 4 | 99.00 | | | | |
| 8- 1 | 98.80 | | | | |
| 8- 2 | 97.75 | | | | |
| 8- 3 | 97.50 | | | | |
| 8- 4 | 96.00 | | | | |
| 8- 5 | 97.50 | | | | |
| 9- 1 | 96.50 | | | | |
| 9- 2 | 96.80 | | | | |
| 9- 3 | 95.00 | | | | |
| 9- 4 | 96.50 | | | | |

## Cycle Wave 5—Bull Market
## Primary Wave 3
## With Intermediate Waves Noted
## S&P 500

| Mo. Wk. # Yr. | | Mo. Wk. # Yr. | | Mo. Wk. # Yr. | |
|---|---|---|---|---|---|
| 3- 2-1978 | 89.00 | 1- 1-1979 | 99.00 | 11- 1 | 101.50 |
| 3- 3 | 90.25 | 1- 2 | 99.80 | 11- 2 | 103.75 |
| 3- 4 | 89.20 | 1- 3 | 99.50 | 11- 3 | 104.90 |
| 3- 5 | 89.10 | 1- 4 | 99.30 | 11- 4 | 106.10 |
| 4- 1 | 90.00 | 1- 5 | 101.75 | 12- 1 | 107.50 |
| 4- 2 | 93.00 | 2- 1 | 97.90 | 12- 2 | 109.00 |
| 4- 3 | 94.25 | 2- 2 | 98.85 | 12- 3 | 107.75 |
| 4- 4 | 97.00 | 2- 3 | 97.75 | 12- 4 | 108.00 |
| 5- 1 | 96.75 | 2- 4 | 97.00 | 1- 1-1980 | 106.50 |
| 5- 2 | 98.00 | 3- 1 | 99.50 | 1- 2 | 109.85 |
| 5- 3 | 98.15 | 3- 2 | 100.80 | 1- 3 | 111.00 |
| 5- 4 | 96.80 | 3- 3 | 101.50 | 1- 4 | 113.50 |
| 5- 5 | 98.25 | 3- 4 | 101.75 | 1- 5 | 115.00 |
| 6- 1 | 99.85 | 4- 1 | 103.50 | 2- 1 | 117.90 * 3 |
| 6- 2 | 97.50 | 4- 2 | 102.00 | 2- 2 | 115.50 |
| 6- 3 | 95.90 | 4- 3 | 101.00 | 2- 3 | 115.00 |
| 6- 4 | 95.50 | 4- 4 | 101.50 | 2- 4 | 113.50 |
| 7- 1 | 95.20 | 5- 1 | 100.85 | 3- 1 | 107.00 |
| 7- 2 | 97.50 | 5- 2 | 98.50 | 3- 2 | 105.50 |
| 7- 3 | 97.75 | 5- 3 | 99.75 | 3- 3 | 102.25 |
| 7- 4 | 100.00 | 5- 4 | 100.20 | 3- 4 | 101.00 |
| 8- 1 | 103.95 | 5- 5 | 99.10 | 4- 1 | 102.00 |
| 8- 2 | 104.00 | 6- 1 | 101.50 | 4- 2 | 103.75 |
| 8- 3 | 105.00 | 6- 2 | 102.00 | 4- 3 | 100.75 * 4 |
| 8- 4 | 105.20 | 6- 3 | 103.00 | 4- 4 | 105.00 |
| 8- 5 | 103.75 | 6- 4 | 103.00 | 4- 5 | 105.50 |
| 9- 1 | 106.90 *1 | 7- 1 | 101.75 | 5- 1 | 104.75 |
| 9- 2 | 104.00 | 7- 2 | 102.25 | 5- 2 | 107.35 |
| 9- 3 | 101.75 | 7- 3 | 101.85 | 5- 3 | 110.75 |
| 9- 4 | 102.75 | 7- 4 | 103.25 | 5- 4 | 111.25 |
| 10- 1 | 103.50 | 8- 1 | 104.00 | 6- 1 | 113.25 |
| 10- 2 | 104.80 | 8- 2 | 106.50 | 6- 2 | 115.75 |
| 10- 3 | 98.00 | 8- 3 | 108.50 | 6- 3 | 114.00 |
| 10- 4 | 94.50 | 8- 4 | 108.75 | 6- 4 | 116.00 |
| 11- 1 | 96.10 | 8- 5 | 109.35 | 7- 1 | 117.50 |
| 11- 2 | 94.70 | 9- 1 | 107.80 | 7- 2 | 117.75 |
| 11- 3 | 94.50 *2 | 9- 2 | 109.00 | 7- 3 | 122.00 |
| 11- 4 | 95.75 | 9- 3 | 110.60 | 7- 4 | 120.75 |
| 11- 5 | 96.40 | 9- 4 | 109.00 | 7- 5 | 121.00 |
| 12= 1 | 96.90 | 10- 1 | 111.25 | 8- 1 | 123.50 |
| 12- 2 | 95.25 | 10- 2 | 104.50 | 8- 2 | 125.75 |
| 12- 3 | 96.50 | 10- 3 | 101.60 | 8- 3 | 126.00 |
| 12- 4 | 96.25 | 10- 4 | 100.80 | 8- 4 | 122.50 |
| | | 10- 5 | 102.50 | 9- 1 | 125.00 |

**Cycle Wave 5—Bull Market**
**Primary Wave 3 (Cont'd)**
**With Intermediate Waves Noted**
**S&P 500**

| Mo. | Wk. # | Yr. | |
|-----|-----|-----|-----|
| 9- | 2 | -80 | 125.50 |
| 9- | 3 | | 129.25 |
| 9- | 4 | | 126.50 |
| 10- | 1 | | 129.30 |
| 10- | 2 | | 130.50 |
| 10- | 3 | | 131.50 |
| 10- | 4 | | 129.90 |
| 10- | 5 | | 127.50 |
| 11- | 1 | | 129.00 |
| 11- | 2 | | 137.00 |
| 11- | 3 | | 139.25 |
| 11- | 4 | | 140.25 |
| 12- | 1 | | 130.00 |
| 12- | 2 | | 133.50 |
| 12- | 3 | | 136.85 |
| 12- | 4 | | 135.50 |
| 1- | 1 | -1981 | 133.50 |
| 1- | 2 | | 135.00 |
| 1- | 3 | | 130.25 |
| 1- | 4 | | 129.50 |
| 1- | 6 | | 140.32***5 |

## Cycle Wave 5—Bear Market
## Primary Wave 4
## With Intermediate Waves Noted
## S&P 500
## (Using Interday Highs & Lows) - Bear Marked 1/6/1981 to 8/9/1982

| Date | New Highs | New Lows | $9.00 Level Direction Reversal Price | Minor Wave Count | $14.00 Level Intermediate Wave Count |
|---|---|---|---|---|---|
| 1- 6-81 | $140.32 | | $131.32 | right shoulder of Bull Top | |
| 1-22-81 | | $129.00 | $138.00 | | |
| 1-23-81 | | 128.50 | 137.50 | | |
| 1-26-81 | | 128.00 | 137.00 | | |
| 2- 2-81 | | 125.75 | 134.75 | | |
| 2-20-81 | | 124.66 | 133.66 | 1 | |
| 3-12-81 | 133.60 | | 124.60 | | |
| 3-13-81 | 135.50 | | 126.50 | | |
| 3-16-81 | 136.25 | | 127.25 | | |
| 3-23-81 | 136.50 | | 127.50 | | |
| 3-24-81 | 137.50 | | 128.50 | | |
| 3-26-81 | 138.38 | | 129.38 | 2 | |
| 5- 5-81 | | 129.30 | 138.30 | | |
| 5-12-81 | | 128.78 | 137.78 | | |
| 6- 3-81 | | 128.50 | 137.50 | | |
| 7- 2-81 | | 127.75 | 136.75 | | |
| 7- 6-81 | | 126.50 | 135.50 | | |
| 7-23-81 | | 125.96 | 134.96 | 3 | |
| 8-12-81 | 135.18 | | 126.18 | 4 | |
| 8-24-81 | | 125.00 | 134.00 | | |
| 8-23-81 | | 124.00 | 133.00 | | |
| 8-31-81 | | 122.50 | 131.50 | | |
| 9- 1-81 | | 121.75 | 130.75 | | |
| 9- 3-81 | | 121.25 | 130.25 | | |
| 9- 4-81 | | 119.00 | 128.00 | | |
| 9- 8-81 | | 117.00 | 126.00 | | |
| 9-18-81 | | 115.50 | 124.50 | | |
| 9-21-81 | | 115.00 | 124.00 | | |
| 9-23-81 | | 113.50 | 122.50 | | |
| 9-25-81 | | 111.64 | 120.64 | 5 | A |
| 10- 2-81 | 120.18 | | 111.18 | | |
| 10- 5-81 | 121.50 | | 112.50 | | |
| 10- 7-81 | 122.00 | | 113.00 | | |
| 10- 8-81 | 122.98 | | 113.98 | | |
| 10- 9-81 | 123.28 | | 114.28 | a | |
| 10-15-81 | | 118.00 | 127.00 | | |
| 10-19-81 | | 117.50 | 126.50 | | |
| 10-26-81 | | 116.81 | 125.81 | b | |
| 11- 3-81 | 125.50 | | 116.50 | | |
| 11- 4-81 | 126.00 | | 117.00 | | |
| 11-30-81 | 127.25 | | 118.25 | | |
| 12- 1-81 | 127.32 | | 118.32 | c | B |

## Cycle Wave 5—Bear Market
## Primary Wave 4 (Cont'd)
## With Intermediate Waves Noted
## S&P 500

| Date | New Highs | New Lows | $9.00 Level Direction Reversal Price | Minor Wave Count | $14.00 Level Intermediate Wave Count |
|---|---|---|---|---|---|
| 1- 6-82 | | $118.00 | $127.00 | | |
| 1- 7-82 | | 117.75 | 126.75 | | |
| 1-11-82 | | 116.75 | 125.75 | | |
| 1-12-82 | | 115.50 | 124.50 | | |
| 1-13-82 | | 114.20 | 123.20 | | |
| 1-14-82 | | 114.00 | 123.00 | | |
| 1-25-82 | | 113.63 | 122.63 | 1 | |
| 1-29-82 | $121.38 | | 116.38 | 2 | ← At this point, |
| 2- 4-82 | | 115.00 | 120.00 | | movements dur- |
| 2- 8-82 | | 114.25 | 119.25 | | ing these waves |
| 2- 9-82 | | 113.00 | 118.00 | | required using |
| 2-16-82 | | 112.20 | 117.20 | | the alternate |
| 2-22-82 | | 111.50 | 116.50 | | Minor Wave |
| 2-23-82 | | 110.00 | 115.00 | 3 | value of $5.00 |
| 2-25-82 | 115.00 | | 110.00 | 4 | |
| 3- 3-82 | | 110.00 | 115.00 | | |
| 3- 4-82 | | 108.50 | 113.50 | | |
| 3- 5-82 | | 107.50 | 112.50 | | |
| 3- 8-82 | | 106.75 | 111.75 | | |
| 3- 9-82 | | 106.17 | 111.17 | 5 | C |
| 4- 2-82 | 116.00 | | 111.00 | | |
| 4- 8-82 | 117.00 | | 112.00 | | |
| 4-13-82 | 117.25 | | 112.25 | | |
| 4-19-82 | 118.00 | | 113.00 | | |
| 4-23-82 | 119.00 | | 114.00 | | |
| 4-26-82 | 120.20 | | 115.20 | a | |
| 4-30-82 | | 115.40 | 120.40 | b | |
| 5- 7-82 | 120.55 | | 115.55 | c | D |
| 6- 1-82 | | 111.25 | 116.25 | | |
| 6- 4-82 | | 109.50 | 114.50 | | |
| 6- 7-82 | | 108.75 | 113.75 | | |
| 6-17-82 | | 107.25 | 112.25 | | |
| 6-18-82 | | 106.33 | 111.33 | 1 | |
| 6-24-82 | 111.50 | | 106.50 | 2 | |
| 7- 8-82 | | 106.18 | 111.18 | 3 | |
| 7-12-82 | 111.20 | | 106.20 | | |
| 7-16-82 | 112.50 | | 107.50 | | |
| 7-21-82 | 113.12 | | 108.12 | 4 | |
| 8- 5-82 | | 104.25 | 109.25 | | |
| 8- 6-82 | | 103.50 | 108.50 | | |
| 8- 9-82 | | 101.44 | 106.44 | 5 | E |

## Cycle Wave 5—Bull Market
## Extended Primary Wave 5
## With Intermediate Waves Noted
## S&P 500
## Extension Included - Bull market 8/9/1982 to 1/1984

| Date | New Highs | New Lows | Direction Reversal Price $9.00 | Minor Wave Count | Intermediate Wave Count |
|---|---|---|---|---|---|
| 8- 9-82 | | $101.44 | $110.44 | Bear Market Low | |
| 8-18-82 | $112.75 | | 103.75 | | |
| 8-20-82 | 113.50 | | 104.50 | | |
| 8-23-82 | 116.25 | | 107.25 | | |
| 8-24-82 | 117.00 | | 108.00 | | |
| 8-26-82 | 121.25 | | 112.25 | | |
| 9- 3-82 | 125.00 | | 116.00 | | |
| 9-16-82 | 125.75 | | 116.75 | | |
| 9-22-82 | 127.31 | | 119.31 | 1 | |
| 10- 1-82 | | 119.13 | 127.13 | 2 | |
| 10- 8-82 | 132.00 | | 123.00 | | |
| 10-11-82 | 136.50 | | 127.50 | | |
| 10-12-82 | 137.00 | | 128.00 | | |
| 10-13-82 | 138.50 | | 129.50 | | |
| 10-20-82 | 140.00 | | 131.00 | | |
| 10-22-82 | 142.00 | | 133.00 | 3 | |
| 10-26-82 | | 131.50 | 140.50 | 4 | |
| 11- 3-82 | 143.50 | | 134.50 | | |
| 11- 4-82 | 145.33 | | 136.33 | 5 | · 1 |
| 11-16-82 | | 133.50 | 142.50 | a ⎫ | Using alternate |
| 11-19-82 | 140.13 | | 135.13 | b ⎬ | Minor Wave |
| 11-23-82 | | 132.09 | 137.09 | c ⎭ | value of $5.00 |
| | | | | | 2 |
| 12- 6-82 | 142.75 | | 133.75 | | |
| 12- 7-82 | 145.00 | | 136.00 | | |
| 1- 6-83 | 146.50 | | 138.00 | | |
| 1- 7-83 | 147.00 | | 138.00 | | |
| 1-10-83 | 148.00 | | 139.00 | | |
| 1-12-83 | 149.08 | | 140.08 | 1 | |
| 1-24-82 | | 137.74 | 146.74 | 2 | |
| 2-10-83 | 148.00 | | 139.00 | | |
| 2-11-83 | 150.00 | | 141.00 | | |
| 2-15-83 | 151.00 | | 142.00 | | |
| 2-25-83 | 152.00 | | 143.00 | | |
| 3- 2-83 | 154.00 | | 145.00 | | |
| 3- 3-82 | 155.03 | | 146.03 | | |
| 4-11-83 | 157.00 | | 148.00 | | |
| 4-14-83 | 160.00 | | 151.00 | | |
| 4-18-83 | 161.00 | | 152.00 | | |
| 4-20-83 | 162.50 | | 153.50 | | |
| 4-21-83 | 163.00 | | 154.00 | | |
| 4-29-83 | 165.00 | | 156.00 | | |
| 5- 6-83 | 167.70 | | 158.70 | 3 | |

## Cycle Wave 5—Bull Market
## Extended Primary Wave 5 (Cont'd)
## With Intermediate Waves Noted
## S&P 500

| Date | New Highs | New Lows | Direction Reversal Price $9.00 | Minor Wave Count | Intermediate Wave Count |
|---|---|---|---|---|---|
| 5-23-83 | | $159.65 | $168.65 | 4 | This wave requir- |
| 6-16-83 | $171.00 | | 162.00 | | ed the alternate |
| 6-21-83 | 171.98 | | 162.98 | | value of $5.00 |
| 6-22-83 | 172.76 | | 163.76 | 5 | 3 |
| 7-18-83 | | 162.48 | 171.48 | a | |
| 7-27-83 | 171.00 | | 162.00 | b | |
| 8- 4-83 | | 159.00 | 168.00 | | |
| 8- 9-83 | | 157.62 | 166.62 | c | 4 |
| 9- 7-83 | 169.00 | | 160.00 | | |
| 9-12-83 | 170.00 | | 161.00 | | |
| 9-23-83 | 171.00 | | 162.00 | | |
| 9-26-83 | 172.00 | | 163.00 | | |
| 10-10-83 | 173.10 | | 164.10 | 1 | |
| 10-28-83 | | 163.00 | 172.00 | | |
| 11- 1-83 | | 161.75 | 170.75 | | |
| 11- 8-83 | | 160.60 | 169.60 | 2 | |
| 11-30-83 | 169.06 | | 160.06 | 3 | |
| 12-16-83 | | 160.60 | 169.60 | 4 | |
| 1- 6-84 | 168.98 | | 160.00 | 5 | 5 |

In November of 1980, while in Intermediate Wave 5, Minor Wave 3 the S&P 500 hit its top price of $141.96. This Bull Market formed a head and shoulders. The right shoulder's price was $140.32, and that was Minor Wave 5, and the end of the Bull Market.

To avoid buying *short* (called a "put" in options) at the lower right shoulder price, I recommend the following: Buy, then sell at Minor Wave 3 of Intermediate Wave 5 at Bull Market tops and at Bear Market bottoms during Intermediate Wave E. This assures greater profits.

Using this strategy, here is a trade-by-trade picture on the S&P 500 for two markets, using the Price Spiral System:

### Bear Market 1/6/1981 to 8/9/1982

|  |  | **Profit** | **Minor #** | **Inter. #** |
|---|---|---|---|---|
| Sell "Short" | 11/1980 at $133.00 |  |  |  |
| Buy Back | 10/2/81 at 120.75 | $12.27 | 5 | A |
| Sell "Short" | 1/6/82 at 118.25 |  |  |  |
| Buy Back | 3/9/82 at 111.25 | $ 7.00 | 5 | C |
| Sell "Short" | 5/7/82 at 115.75 |  |  |  |
| Buy Back | 7/9/82 at 106.50 | $ 9.25 | 3 | E |
|  |  | $28.52 |  |  |

Summary: 3 Trades,
Summary: 3 Trades, 3 Profits, <u>0</u> Losses!

---

### Bull Market 8/9/1982 to 1/1984

|  |  | **Profit** | **Minor #** | **Inter. #** |
|---|---|---|---|---|
| Buy "Long" | 8/ 9/82 at $106.50 |  |  |  |
| Sell | 11/ 4/82 at 136.50 | $30.00 | 5 | 1 |
| Buy "Long" | 11/23/82 at 137.20 |  |  |  |
| Sell | 6/22/83 at 163.80 | $26.60 | 5 | 3 |
| Buy "Long" | 8/ 9/83 at 166.80 |  |  |  |
| Sell | 11/30/83 at 169.00 | $ 2.20 | 3 | 5 |
|  |  | $58.00 |  |  |

Summary: 3 Trades, 3 Profits, 0 Losses!

## Cycle Wave 5
## Extension Bear Market
## Primary Wave 5 (Cont'd)
## S&P 500
## Bear Market January 6, 1984 to July 20, 1984—Extension 6

The data for Intermediate Wave 1 was not available to me. However, I have included the charts showing this time period, with the Minor Wave noted.

I then start applying the Spiral System to the S&P 500 at the end of Intermediate Wave 1 on through to the present time.

```
       Date

1/ 6/84        $168.98                Bull Top
  1/13          167.00
    20          169.00
    27          163.80
2/ 3            156.10
    10          155.90
    17          157.25
    24          159.10
3/ 2            154.25    ***A  _____
     9          159.00
    16          156.75          NOTE ***Data based on a
    23          159.00               WEEKLY average.
    30          155.20
4/ 6            157.25
    13          158.10
    20          159.75    ***B  _____
    27          159.00
5/ 4            158.50
    11          155.75
    18          154.25
    25          153.00
6/ 1            155.00
     8          149.00
    15          154.40
    22          154.00
    29          152.10
7/ 6            151.00
    13          149.25    ***C
```

108

**Cycle Wave 5—Current Bull Market**
**Extended Primary Wave 5 (Cont'd)**
**S&P 500**
**July 14, 1984 to Present**

The data for Intermediate Wave 1 was not available to me. However, I have included the charts showing this time period, with the Minor Wave noted.

I then start applying the Spiral System to the S&P 500 at the end of Intermediate Wave 1 on through to the present time.

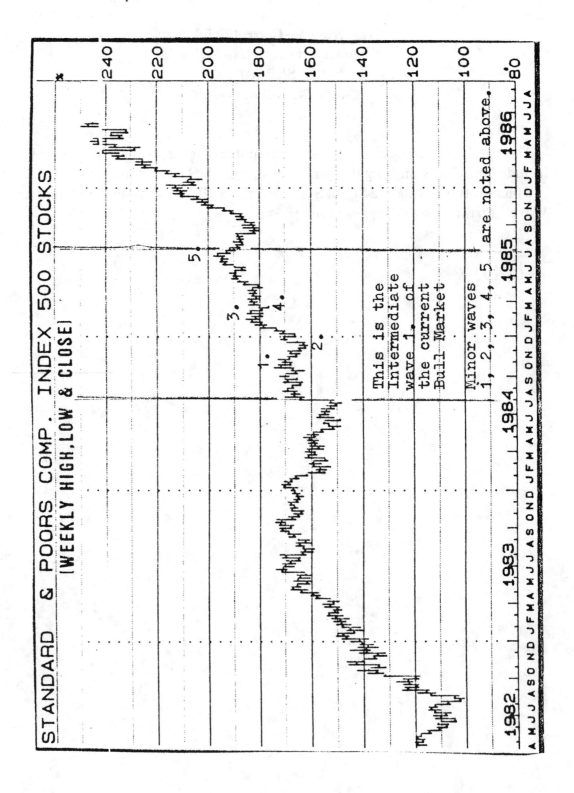

STANDARD & POORS COMP. INDEX 500 STOCKS
(WEEKLY HIGH,LOW & CLOSE)

This is the
Intermediate
wave 1. of
the current
Bull Market

Minor waves
1, 2, 3, 4, 5  are noted above.

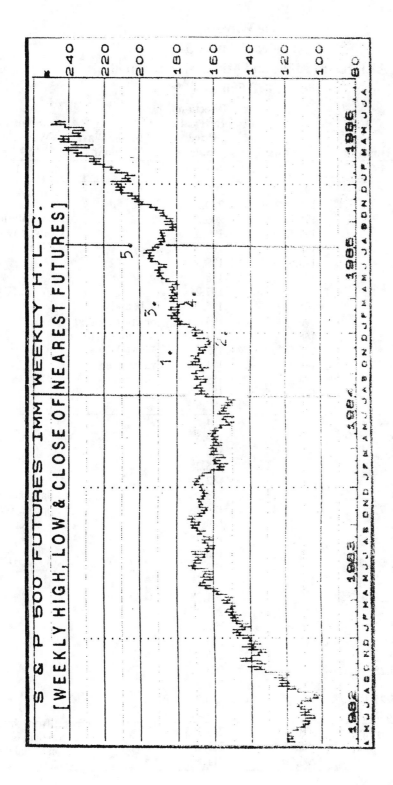

**Cycle Wave 5**
**Extended Primary 5**
**ALL Intermediate and Minor Waves Noted**
**S&P 500**

| Date | New Highs | New Lows | Direction Reversal Price $5.00 | Minor Wave Count | Intermediate Wave Count $9.00 |
|---|---|---|---|---|---|
| 7-18-85 | 203.5 | | 198.5 | 5 | 1 |
| 7-24-85 | | 197.75 | 202.75 | | |
| 7-29-85 | | 195.375 | 200.375 | | |
| 7-30-85 | | 195.25 | 200.25 | | See Alternate |
| 8- 6-85 | | 194.5 | 199.5 | | Minor Wave |
| 8-12-85 | | 194 | 199 | | Chart on Pg. 115 |
| 8-16-85 | | 193.5 | 198.5 | | |
| 8-15-85 | | 193 | 198 | | |
| 8-16-85 | | 192.25 | 197.25 | | |
| 9- 4-85 | | 191 | 196 | a, b, and c | |
| 9-10-85 | | 190 | 195 | reactions found | |
| 9-11-85 | | 188.25 | 193.25 | with alternate | |
| 9-12-85 | | 187.5 | 192.5 | Minor Wave | |
| 9-13-85 | | 186.5 | 191.5 | value—see | |
| 9-17-85 | | 184 | 189 | alternate | |
| 9-25-85 | | 183 | 188 | chart. | |
| 9-26-85 | | 182.5 | 187.5 | | 2 |
| 10-14-85 | 189 | | 184 | | |
| 10-16-85 | 189.5 | | 184.5 | | |
| 10-23-85 | 191 | | 186 | | |
| 10-29-85 | 191.25 | | 186.25 | | |
| 10-30-85 | 192 | | 187 | | |
| 11- 1-85 | 193 | | 188 | | data base *** |
| 11- 5-85 | 193.75 | | 188.75 | | approx. Weekly |
| 11- 6-85 | 194 | | 189 | | Average |
| 11-11-85 | 199.75 | | 194.75 | | |
| 11-12-85 | 201 | | 196 | | |
| 11-14-85 | 202 | | 198 | | |
| 11-21-85 | 204 | | 199 | | |
| 11-27-85 | 206.25 | | 201.25 | | |
| 12- 4-85 | 207.375 | | 202.375 | | |
| 12- 9-85 | 207.625 | | 202.625 | | |
| 12-10-85 | 208 | | 203 | | |
| 12-11-85 | 210 | | 205 | | |
| 12-12-85 | 210.25 | | 205.25 | | |
| 12-13-85 | 213.5 | | 208.5 | | |
| 12-16-85 | 215.25 | | 210.25 | | |
| 1- 7-86 | 216.25 | | 211.25 | 1 | |
| 1- 8-86 | | 208.375 | 213.375 | | ...from this point on data is based |
| 1- 9-86 | | 206.75 | 211.75 | | on actual daily |
| 1-10-86 | | 206.50 | 211.50 | 2 | close |

112

## Cycle Wave 5
## Extended Primary 5 (Cont'd)
## ALL Intermediate and Minor Waves Noted
## S&P 500

| Date | New Highs | New Lows | Direction Reversal Price $5.00 | Minor Wave Count | Intermediate Wave Count $9.00 | |
|---|---|---|---|---|---|---|
| 1-28-86 | 212.10 | | 207.10 | | | |
| 1-31-86 | 213.00 | | 208.00 | | | |
| 2-14-86 | 219.76 | | 214.76 | | | |
| 2-18-86 | 222.45 | | 217.45 | | | |
| 2-21-86 | 225 | | 220 | | | |
| 2-27-86 | 227 | | 222 | | | |
| 3-11-86 | 232 | | 227 | | | |
| 3-12-86 | 233 | | 228 | | | |
| 3-14-86 | 237 | | 232 | | | |
| 3-27-86 | 239 | | 230 | 3 | | |
| 4- 4-86 | | 229 | 238 | | | |
| 4- 7-86 | | 229 | 238 | 4 | | |
| 4-15-86 | 238 | | 229 | | | |
| 4-16-86 | 242 | | 233 | | | |
| 4-17-86 | 243 | | 234 | | | |
| 4-21-86 | 245 | | 236 | 5 | 3 | |
| 4-30-86 | | 236 | 245 | | | |
| 5- 1-86 | | 235 | 244 | | | |
| 5-15-86 | | 234 | 243 | | | |
| 5-16-86 | | 233 | 247 | ..........a,b,c.......... | 4... | because of the gain so far in this bull market we shall raise the Minor Wave p/r level here to $14.00 |
| 5-27-86 | 247 | | 233 | | | |
| 6-20-86 | 248 | | 234 | | | |
| 6-25-86 | 249 | | 235 | | | |
| 6-27-86 | 250 | | 236 | | | |
| 6-30-86 | 251 | | 237 | | | |
| 7- 1-86 | 252 | | 238 | | | |
| 7- 2-86 | 253 | | 239 | 1 | | |
| 7-14-86 | | 238 | 252 | | | |
| 7-15-86 | | 234 | 248 | 2 | | |
| 8-20-86 | 250 | | 236 | | | |
| 8-26-86 | 253 | | 239 | | | |
| 9- 4-86 | 254 | | 240 | 3 | | |
| 9-11-86 | | 235 | 249 | | | The Intermediate Wave level is $24.00, and although the total loss on this Minor Wave was $24.00, it still is a Minor Wave 4 ONLY. We know that the 5th wave is yet to develop. |
| 9-12-86 | | 231 | 245 | | | |
| 9-29-86 | | 230 | 244 | 4 | | |
| 10-30-86 | 244 | | 230 | | | |
| 11- 3-86 | 246 | | 232 | | | |
| 11- 5-86 | 247 | | 233 | | | |
| 11-25-86 | 248 | | 234 | | | |
| 11-28-86 | 249 | | 235 | | | |

## Cycle Wave 5
## Extended Primary Wave 5 (Cont'd)
## ALL Intermediate and Minor Waves Noted
## S&P 500

| Date | New Highs | New Lows | Direction Reversal Price $5.00 | Minor Wave Count | Intermediate Wave Count $9.00 |
|------|-----------|----------|-------------------------------|------------------|-------------------------------|
| 12- 2-86 | 249 | | 240 | | |
| 1- 7-87 | 254 | | 241 | | |
| 1- 8-87 | 257 | | 243 | | |
| 1- 9-87 | 259 | | 245 | | |
| 1-12-87 | 260 | | 246 | | |
| 1-14-87 | 263 | | 249 | | |
| 1-15-87 | 265 | | 251 | | |
| 1-16-87 | 266 | | 252 | | |
| 1-19-87 | 269 | | 255 | | |
| 1-22-87 | 274 | | 260 | | |
| 1-28-87 | 275 | | 261 | | |
| 2- 2-87 | 276 | | 262 | | |
| 2- 4-87 | 280 | | 266 | | |
| 2- 5-87 | 281 | | 267 | | |
| 2-17-87 | 285 | | 271 | | |
| 2-19-87 | 286 | | 272 | | |
| 3- 4-87 | 289 | | 275 | | |
| 3- 5-87 | 291 | | 277 | | |
| 3-17-87 | 292 | | 278 | | |
| 3-18-87 | 293 | | 279 | | |
| 3-19-87 | 294 | | 280 | | |
| 3-20-87 | 298 | | 284 | | |
| 3-23-87 | 301 | | 287 | | |
| 3-24-87 | 302 | | 288 | | |
| 4- 6-87 | 302 | | 288 | 5 | |
| 4-13-87 | | 286 | 300 | | |
| 4-14-87 | | 279 | 293 | ext 6 | |
| 4-21-87 | 293 | | 279 | | |
| 5- 5-87 | 295 | | 281 | ext 7 | |
| 5-19-87 | | 280 | 294 | | |
| 5-20-87 | | 278 | 292 | ext 8 | |
| 6- 3-87 | 293 | | 279 | | |
| 6- 5-87 | 295 | | 281 | | |
| 6- 8-87 | 297 | | 283 | | |
| 6-11-87 | 299 | | 285 | | |
| 6-12-87 | 302 | | 288 | | |
| 6-15-87 | 303 | | 289 | | |
| 6-16-87 | 305 | | 291 | ext 9 | |
| 6-18-87 | 306 | | 292 | | |
| 6-19-87 | 307 | | 293 | in | |
| 6-22-87 | 310 | | 296 | progress! | |

*Note:* The loss on this Minor Wave was $23.00—*Not* enough to register on the $24.00 Intermediate Wave that this Bull Market had ended.

114

## Alternate Minor Wave Chart
## S&P 500

| Date | New Highs | New Lows | Direction Reversal Price | Minor Waves Using Alternate $3.00 | Intermediate Wave $9.00 |
|---|---|---|---|---|---|
| 7-18-85 | 203.5 | | 200.5 | 5 | 3 |
| 7-23-85 | | 199 | 202 | | |
| 7-24-85 | | 197.75 | 200.75 | | |
| 7-29-85 | | 195.375 | 198.375 | | |
| 7-30-85 | | 195.25 | 198.25 | | |
| 8- 8-85 | | 194.5 | 197.5 | | |
| 8- 9-85 | | 194 | 197 | | |
| 8-12-85 | | 193.5 | 196.5 | | |
| 8-15-85 | | 193 | 196 | | |
| 8-16-85 | | 192.25 | 195.25 | a | |
| 8-20-85 | 195.5 | | 192.5 | b | |
| 8-30-85 | | 192.25 | 195.25 | | |
| 9- 4-85 | | 191 | 194 | | |
| 9-10-85 | | 190 | 193 | | |
| 9-11-85 | | 188.25 | 191.25 | | |
| 9-12-85 | | 187.5 | 190.5 | | |
| 9-13-85 | | 186.5 | 189.5 | | |
| 9-17-85 | | 184 | 187 | c | |
| 9-23-85 | 188 | | 184 | d | |
| 9-25-85 | | 183 | 186 | | |
| 9-26-85 | | 182.5 | 185.5 | e | 4 |

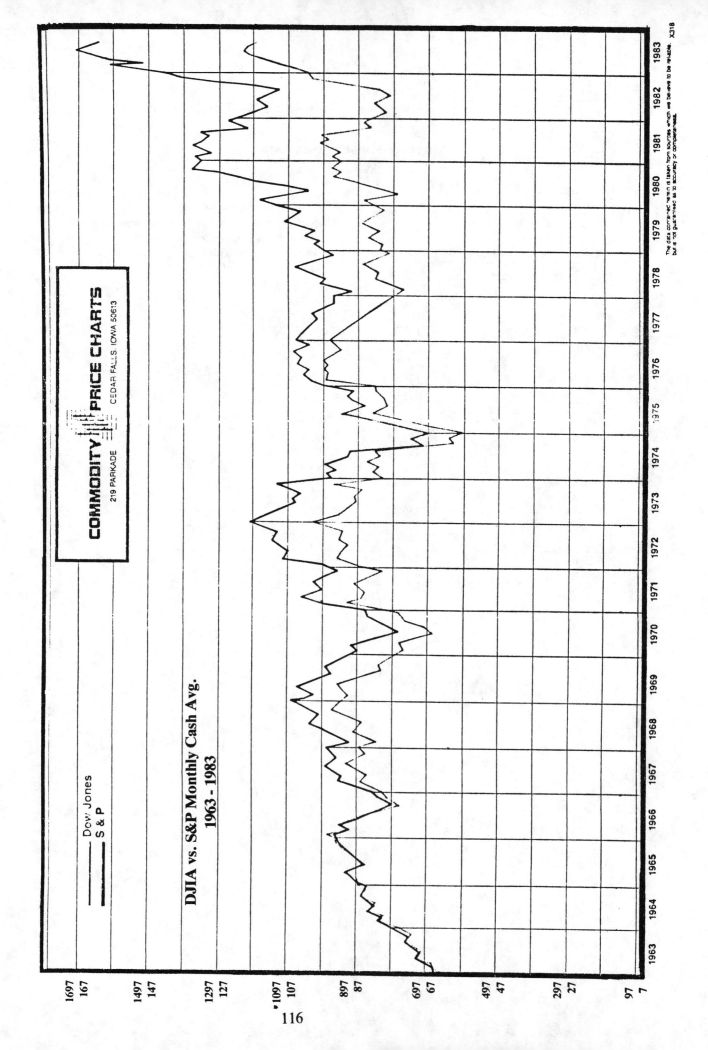

COMMODITY PRICE CHARTS
219 PARKADE    CEDAR FALLS, IOWA 50613

DJIA vs. S&P Monthly Cash Avg.
1963 - 1983

Dow Jones
S & P

The data contained herein is taken from sources which we believe to be reliable, but is not guaranteed as to accuracy or completeness.    X318

116

# Part III
# HISTORY OF THE STOCK MARKET CYCLES

## Applying the Price Spiral System
## To the Sept. S&P Futures Contract
## Period—June 3, 1987 to June 12, 1987

In this example, we will be "Tracking" *Minute Waves*, which are only found in hourly data. This is a perfect example of what I call "Super-Timing." That is, when one uses the smaller waves to build into the next larger wave patterns. This method is especially useful in timing Fifth Wave turning points.

On the next page is a chart showing how each wave classification builds and completes to form the next higher wave division.

## INTERMEDIATE WAVES = 5

| 1 | 1 | 1 | 1 | 1 |
|---|---|---|---|---|
| | 1 | 2 | 3 4 | 5 |

## MINOR WAVES = 21

| 1 | 2 | 3 | 4 | 5 | a | b | c | 1 | 2 | 3 | 4 | 5 | a | b | c | 1 | 2 | 3 | 4 | 5 |
|---|---|---|---|---|---|---|---|---|---|---|---|---|---|---|---|---|---|---|---|---|
| 5 | | | | | 3 | | | 5 | | | | | 3 | | | 5 | | | | |

5   8   13   16   21

## MINUTE WAVES = 89

| 5 | 3 | 5 | 3 | 5 | 5 | 3 | 5 | 5 | 3 | 5 | 3 | 5 | 5 | 3 | 5 | 5 | 3 | 5 | 3 | 5 |
|---|---|---|---|---|---|---|---|---|---|---|---|---|---|---|---|---|---|---|---|---|
| | | | | | a | b | c | | | | | | a | b | c | | | | | (X) |

21   34   55   68   89

## MINUTE WAVES (HOURLY DATA) = 377

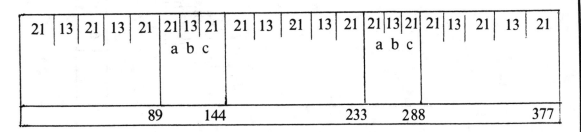

| 21 | 13 | 21 | 13 | 21 | 21 | 13 | 21 | 21 | 13 | 21 | 13 | 21 | 21 | 13 | 21 | 21 | 13 | 21 | 13 | 21 |
|----|----|----|----|----|----|----|----|----|----|----|----|----|----|----|----|----|----|----|----|----|
| | | | | | a | b | c | | | | | | a | b | c | | | | | |

89   144   233   288   377

*Note:* Area marked above with "X" shows the ideal time to super-time the system, by keeping track of the minute wave pattern.

119

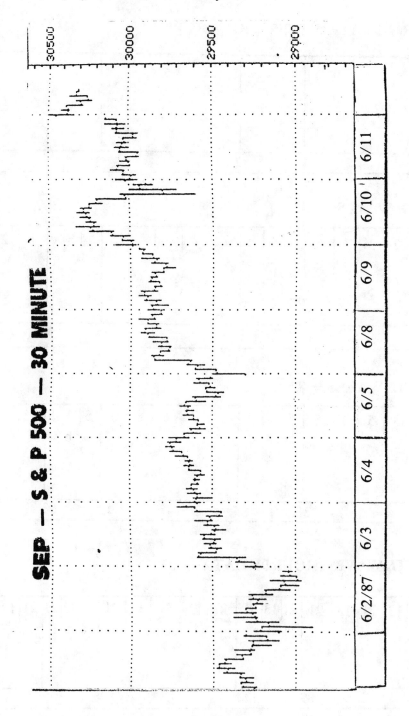

## Intra-Day Trading

| Date | Time | New Highs | New Lows | Direction Reversal Level $2.40 (.236) | Sub-Minute Wave Count |
|------|------|-----------|----------|---------------------------------------|------------------------|
| 6- 2-87 | 3:00PM | | 289.7 | 292.1 | low of down move...... |
| 6- 3-87 | 9:30AM | 292.5 | | 290.1 | |
| | 10:00AM | 293.35 | | 290.9 | |
| | 10:30AM | 295.80 | | 293.4 | |
| | 3:30PM | 296.00 | | 293.6 | |
| | 4:00PM | 296.50 | | 294.1 | |
| 6- 4-87 | 2:30PM | 296.60 | | 294.2 | |
| | 3:00PM | 297.20 | | 294.8 | |
| | 3:30PM | 297.25 | | 294.85 | 1 |
| 6- 5-87 | 2:00PM | | 294.75 | 297.1 | |
| | 2:30PM | | 294.60 | 297.0 | 2 |
| 6- 8-87 | 11:00AM | 298.50 | | 296.1 | |
| | 1:30PM | 298.80 | | 296.4 | |
| | 2:00PM | 299.10 | | 296.7 | |
| 6- 9-87 | 11:00AM | 299.25 | | 296.8 | |
| | 4:00PM | 299.45 | | 297.0 | |
| 6-10-87 | 9:30AM | 299.80 | | 297.4 | |
| | 10:00AM | 300.50 | | 298.1 | |
| | 10:30AM | 301.00 | | 298.6 | |
| | 11:00AM | 302.30 | | 299.9 | |
| | 12:30PM | 302.65 | | 300.2 | 3 |
| | 2:30PM | | 300.25 | 302.6 | |
| | 3:00PM | | 297.90 | 300.3 | 4 |
| 6-11-87 | 10:00AM | 300.40 | | 298.0 | |
| | 10:30AM | 300.65 | | 298.2 | |
| | 2:00PM | 300.75 | | 298.4 | |
| 6-11-87 | 4:00PM | 301.50 | | 299.1 | |
| 6-12-87 | 9:30AM | 303.75 | | 301.4 | 5 |

Buying in on this move at $292.10 and selling at $301.40 would have gained a *sure* profit of $9.30 per contract for the 8 day period!

## Dow Jones Industrials
## Current Bull Market 7/24/84 to Present
## Cycle Wave 5
## Primary Wave 5
## *All* Intermediate and Minor Waves Noted

| Date | New Highs | New Lows | Direction Reversal Level $38.00 | Minor Wave Count | Intermediate Wave Count |
|---|---|---|---|---|---|
| 7-24-84 | | $1087 | $1111 | Bear Move Bottom | |
| 7-27-84 | $1115 | | 1077 | | |
| 8- 7-84 | 1205 | | 1167 | | |
| 8- 9-84 | 1224 | | 1186 | | |
| 8-21-84 | 1240 | | 1202 | 1 | |
| 9-10-84 | | 1202 | 1240 | | |
| 9-11-84 | | 1198 | 1236 | 2 | |
| 9-14-84 | 1238 | | 1200 | 3 | |
| 10- 1-84 | | 1199 | 1237 | | |
| 10- 2-84 | | 1191 | 1229 | | |
| 10- 3-84 | | 1183 | 1221 | | |
| 10- 9-84 | | 1175 | 1213 | 4 | |
| 10-18-84 | 1225 | | 1187 | | |
| 10-19-84 | 1226 | | 1188 | | |
| 11- 5-84 | 1229 | | 1191 | | |
| 11- 6-84 | 1244 | | 1206 | 5 | 1 |
| 11-15-84 | | 1206 | 1244 | | |
| 11-16-84 | | 1188 | 1226 | | |
| 11-19-84 | | 1185 | 1223 | | |
| 12- 3-84 | | 1182 | 1220 | (see Minute Wave Chart) | |
| 12- 5-84 | | 1172 | 1210 | | |
| 12- 6-84 | | 1170 | 1208 | | |
| 12- 7-84 | | 1163 | 1201 | A,B,C, | 2 |
| 12-18-84 | 1212 | | 1174 | | |
| 1-10-85 | 1224 | | 1186 | | |
| 1-14-85 | 1235 | | 1197 | | |
| 1-21-85 | 1261 | | 1223 | | |
| 1-23-85 | 1275 | | 1237 | | |
| 1-25-85 | 1276 | | 1238 | | |
| 1-28-85 | 1278 | | 1240 | | |
| 1-29-85 | 1293 | | 1255 | | |
| 2-13-85 | 1298 | | 1260 | | |
| 3- 1-85 | 1299 | | 1261 | | |
| 5-20-85 | 1305 | | 1243 ⟵·············· | | |

At this point we shall raise the Minor Wave level to $62.00, as we have surpassed the $1287 top of 1984.

122

**Dow Jones Industrials**
**Current Bull Market 7/24/84 to Present (Cont'd)**

| Date | New Highs | New Lows | Direction Reversal Level $38.00 | Minor Wave Count | Intermediate Wave Count |
|------|-----------|----------|--------------------------------|------------------|-------------------------|
| 5-21-85 | 1310 | | 1248 | | |
| 5-31-85 | 1315 | | 1253 | | |
| 6- 5-85 | 1321 | | 1259 | | |
| 6- 6-85 | 1327 | | 1265 | | |
| 6-27-85 | 1332 | | 1270 | | |
| 6-28-85 | 1335 | | 1273 | | |
| 7- 1-85 | 1337 | | 1275 | | |
| 7-11-85 | 1338 | | 1276 | | |
| 7-12-85 | 1339 | | 1277 | | |
| 7-16-85 | 1348 | | 1286 | | |
| 7-17-85 | 1358 | | 1296 | | |
| 7-19-85 | 1360 | | 1298 | | |

Between 7-19-85 and 10-16-85, the Dow Jones Industrials neither rose nor fell, but stayed in the range between 1360 and 1298.

## Dow Jones Industrials
## Current Bull Market 7/24/84 to Present (Cont'd)

| Date | New Highs | New Lows | Direction Reversal Level $62.00 | Minor Wave Count | Intermediate Wave Count |
|---|---|---|---|---|---|
| 10-16-85 | $1369 | | $1307 | | |
| 10-30-85 | 1376 | | 1314 | | |
| 11- 1-85 | 1390 | | 1328 | | |
| 11- 5-85 | 1397 | | 1335 | | |
| 11- 6-85 | 1403 | | 1341 | | |
| 11- 8-85 | 1404 | | 1342 | | |
| 11-11-85 | 1432 | | 1370 | | |
| 11-12-85 | 1434 | | 1372 | | |
| 11-14-85 | 1439 | | 1377 | | |
| 11-18-85 | 1440 | | 1378 | | |
| 11-21-85 | 1462 | | 1400 | | |
| 11-22-85 | 1464 | | 1402 | | |
| 11-27-85 | 1476 | | 1414 | | |
| 12- 4-85 | 1484 | | 1422 | | |
| 12- 9-85 | 1497 | | 1435 | | |
| 12-10-85 | 1499 | | 1437 | | |
| 12-11-85 | 1512 | | 1450 | | |
| 12-13-85 | 1535 | | 1473 | | |
| 12-16-85 | 1553 | | 1491 | | |
| 1- 7-86 | 1566 | | 1504 | 1 | |
| 1-22-86 | | $1502 | 1566 | 2 | |
| 1-31-86 | 1571 | | 1509 | | |
| 2- 3-86 | 1594 | | 1532 | | |
| 2- 6-85 | 1601 | | 1539 | | |
| 2- 7-86 | 1613 | | 1551 | | |
| 2-10-86 | 1626 | | 1564 | | |
| 2-12-86 | 1630 | | 1568 | | |
| 2-13-86 | 1645 | | 1583 | | |
| 2-14-86 | 1664 | | 1602 | | |
| 2-18-85 | 1679 | | 1617 | | |
| 2-21-86 | 1698 | | 1636 | | |
| 2-27-86 | 1714 | | 1652 | | |
| 3-11-86 | 1746 | | 1684 | | |
| 3-13-86 | 1754 | | 1692 | | |
| 3-14-86 | 1793 | | 1731 | | |
| 3-20-86 | 1804 | | 1742 | | |
| 3-26-86 | 1811 | | 1749 | | |
| 3-27-86 | 1822 | | 1760 | 3 | |
| 4- 4-86 | | 1739 | 1801 | | |
| 4- 7-86 | | 1736 | 1798 | 4 | |
| 4-14-86 | 1805 | | 1743 | | |
| 4-15-86 | 1810 | | 1748 | | |
| 4-16-86 | 1845 | | 1783 | | |
| 4-17-86 | 1855 | | 1793 | | |
| 4-21-86 | 1856 | | 1794 | 5 | 3 |

## Dow Jones Industrials
## Current Bull Market 7/24/84 to Present (Cont'd)

| Date | New Highs | New Lows | Direction Reversal Level $62.00 | Minor Wave Count | Intermediate Wave Count |
|---|---|---|---|---|---|
| 4-30-86 | | $1784 | $1846 | | The b Wave here occurred during the intra-day trading on May 14, posting a $23.00 gain on the close of $1808.00. |
| 5- 1-86 | | 1778 | 1840 | | |
| 5- 2-86 | | 1775 | 1837 | | |
| 5-16-86 | | 1760 | 1822 | | |
| 5-19-86 | | 1758 | 1858 | A,B,C | |
| 5-28-86 | $1878 | | 1778 | | Because of the strength of this Bull Market and since the loss on Intermediate Wave 4 was so near the next highest dollar value of *$100.00*, we shall at this point again raise the Minor Wave value amount. |
| 5-29-86 | 1882 | | 1782 | | |
| 6- 6-86 | 1886 | | 1786 | | |
| 6-30-86 | 1893 | | 1793 | | |
| 7- 1-86 | 1904 | | 1804 | | |
| 7- 2-86 | 1909 | | 1809 | 1 | |
| 7-14-86 | | 1793 | 1893 | | |
| 7-15-86 | | 1769 | 1869 | | |
| 7-29-86 | | 1767 | 1867 | | |
| 8- 1-86 | | 1764 | 1864 | 2 | |
| 8-18-86 | 1870 | | 1770 | | |
| 8-20-86 | 1881 | | 1781 | | |
| 8-22-86 | 1888 | | 1788 | | |
| 8-26-86 | 1904 | | 1804 | | |
| 8-27-86 | 1905 | | 1805 | | |
| 9- 4-86 | 1920 | | 1820 | 3 | |
| 9-11-86 | | 1793 | 1893 | | |
| 9-12-86 | | 1759 | 1859 | | |
| 9-29-86 | | 1755 | 1855 | 4 | Although the total loss on Minor Wave 4 amounted to more than the $162.00 value for waves on the Intermediate Wave Level— this *was* very close to that amount and it was still only the 4th Minor Wave. We knew that the 5th Wave was yet to come and we had not yet reached the peak of this great Bull Market.... |
| 10-30-86 | 1878 | | 1778 | | |
| 11- 3-86 | 1894 | | 1794 | | |
| 11- 5-86 | 1899 | | 1799 | | |
| 11-24-86 | 1906 | | 1806 | | |
| 11-25-86 | 1912 | | 1812 | | |
| 11-26-86 | 1917 | | 1817 | | |
| 12- 2-87 | 1956 | | 1856 | | |
| 1- 5-87 | 1971 | | 1871 | | |
| 1- 6-87 | 1975 | | 1875 | | |
| 1- 7-87 | 1994 | | 1894 | | |
| 1- 8-87 | 2002 | | 1902 | | |
| 1- 9-87 | 2006 | | 1906 | | |
| 1-12-87 | 2009 | | 1909 | | |
| 1-13-87 | 2013 | | 1913 | | |
| 1-14-87 | 2035 | | 1935 | | |
| 1-15-87 | 2071 | | 1971 | | |
| 1-16-87 | 2077 | | 1977 | | |
| 1-19-87 | 2103 | | 2003 | | |
| 1-20-87 | 2104 | | 2004 | | |
| 1-22-87 | 2146 | | 2046 | | |
| 1-27-87 | 2150 | | 2050 | | |
| 1-28-87 | 2163 | | 2063 | | |

## Dow Jones Industrials
## Current Bull Market 7/24/84 to Present (Cont'd)

| Date | New Highs | New Lows | Direction Reversal Level $62.00 | Minor Wave Count | Intermediate Wave Count |
|------|-----------|----------|----------------------------------|------------------|-------------------------|
| 2- 2-87 | $2179 | | $2079 | | |
| 2- 4-87 | 2191 | | 2091 | | |
| 2- 5-87 | 2201 | | 2101 | | |
| 2-17-87 | 2237 | | 2137 | | |
| 2-18-87 | 2238 | | 2138 | | |
| 2-19-87 | 2244 | | 2144 | | |
| 3- 4-87 | 2257 | | 2157 | | |
| 3- 5-87 | 2276 | | 2176 | | |
| 3- 6-87 | 2280 | | 2180 | | |
| 3-17-87 | 2285 | | 2185 | | |
| 3-18-87 | 2287 | | 2187 | | |
| 3-19-87 | 2300 | | 2200 | | |
| 3-20-87 | 2334 | | 2234 | | |
| 3-23-87 | 2364 | | 2264 | | |
| 3-24-87 | 2369 | | 2269 | | |
| 3-26-87 | 2373 | | 2273 | | |
| 4- 3-87 | 2390 | | 2290 | | |
| 4- 6-87 | 2405 | | 2305 | 5 | |
| 4-13-87 | | $2287 | $2387 | | |
| 4-14-87 | | 2253 | 2353 | | |
| 4-24-87 | | 2235 | 2335 | ext. 6 | |
| 6- 4-87 | 2337 | | 2237 | | |
| 6- 8-87 | 2352 | | 2252 | | |
| 6- 9-87 | 2353 | | 2253 | | |
| 6-10-87 | 2354 | | 2254 | | |
| 6-11-87 | 2360 | | 2260 | | |
| 6-12-87 | 2378 | | 2278 | | |
| 6-15-87 | 2392 | | 2292 | | |
| 6-16-87 | 2407 | | 2307 | ext. 7... | |
| 6-18-87 | 2408 | | 2308 | in | |
| 6-19-87 | 2421 | | 2321 | progress! | |
| 6-22-87 | 2446 | | 2346 | | |
| 6-25-87 | 2451 | | 2351 | | |

*Note:* A Bear move is due to follow soon. One must be very alert to its meaning. *If* the loss is of $250.00 or more points on the first wave down, then chances are excellent that we are in a full fledged Bear Market. However, *if* the loss is under $200.00—we then may look for an *insufficient* correction, with yet another extension *up* to follow.

The same will hold true for the S&P 500, only on a smaller point loss of between $30.00 to $38.00.

**Minute Wave Chart**
**(For 11/6/84 to 12/11/84 Only)**

| Date | New Highs | New Lows | Direction Reversal Level $15.00 | Minute Wave Count | Minor Wave Count |
|---|---|---|---|---|---|
| 11- 6-84 | $1244 | | $1229 | | 5 |
| 11- 8-84 | | $1229 | 1244 | | |
| 11- 9-84 | | 1219 | 1234 | | |
| 11-13-84 | | 1207 | 1222 | | |
| 11-19-84 | | 1185 | 1200 | A | |
| 11-23-84 | 1220 | | 1205 | B | |
| 11-28-84 | | 1205 | 1220 | | |
| 12- 3-84 | | 1182 | 1197 | | |
| 12- 7-84 | | 1163 | 1178 | C | A,B,C |
| 12-11-84 | 1178 | | | | |

127

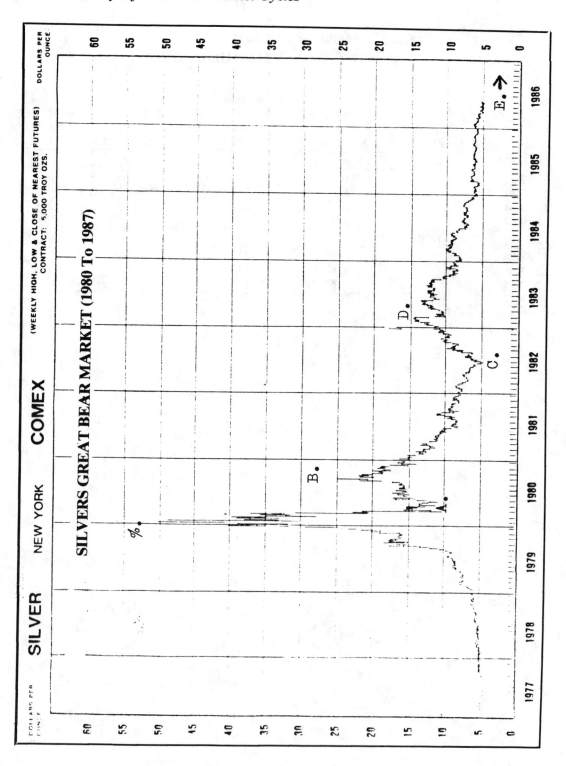

The chart on the previous page is the long term chart for Silver - Comex. We can see that the great Bear Market which began in January 1980 is one of the classic examples of our 5 wave pattern. Silver continued its decline, tapering off to its final low which occurred in late December of 1986.

On the following two pages are 2 charts for Comex Silver—one for July, 1987 and the second for December, 1987. It is quite clear that these two charts *show* the first 2 Minor Waves in a new Bull Market for Silver, when you place the up move to 10 on the preceding chart.

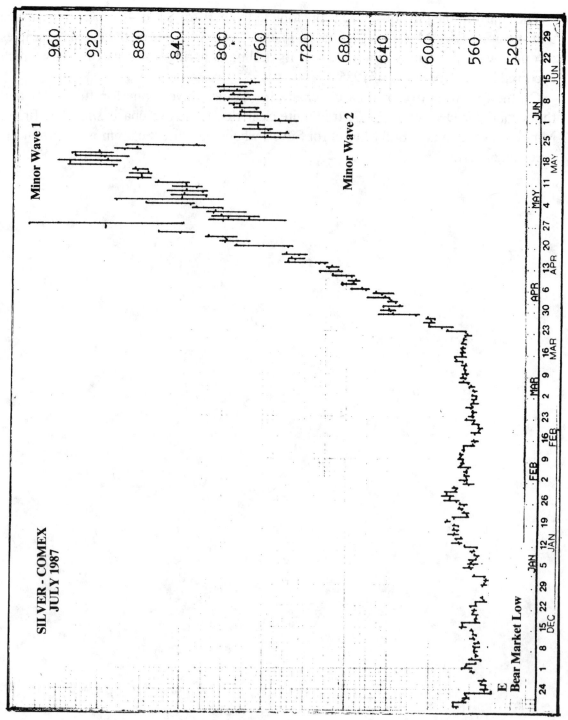

SILVER - COMEX
JULY 1987

Minor Wave 1

Minor Wave 2

Bear Market Low

For those who are interested in "tracking" Silver, I have set the Price Spiral dollar values at:

| Ratio Value | Converted Dollar Value | |
|---|---|---|
| .236 | $2.40 | Minor Waves |
| .382 | $3.80 | Intermediate Waves |

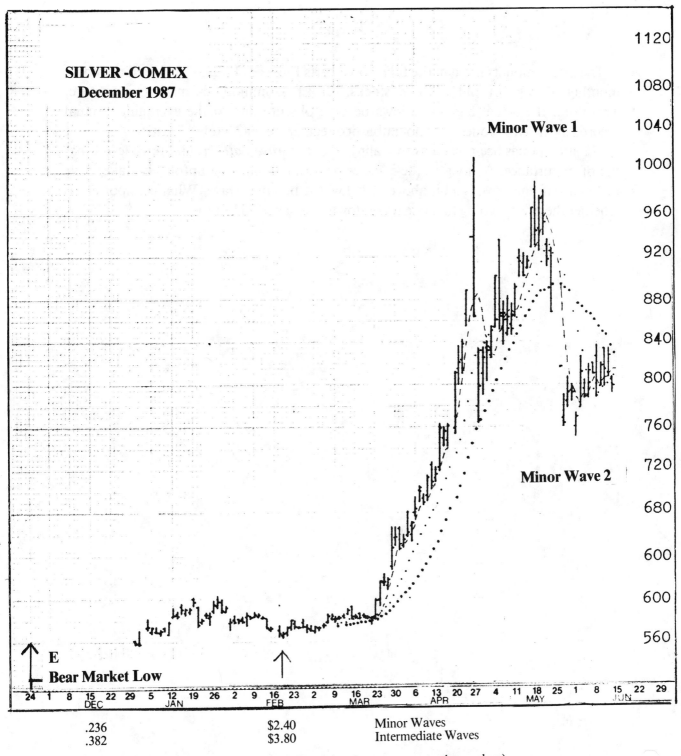

**SILVER -COMEX**
**December 1987**

Minor Wave 1

Minor Wave 2

E
**Bear Market Low**

| | | | |
|---|---|---|---|
| .236 | $2.40 | Minor Waves | |
| .382 | $3.80 | Intermediate Waves | |

(Of course, as this move progresses adjustments may become necessary to these values).

131

## NOTE

The price amounts listed in the following charts for years 1702 to 1885 are based on a monthly average of old railroad stocks, British Commodities markets, etc., etc. Therefore, the actual highs and lows become obscure due to the averaging. Actual records of the Dow Jones were not published regularly until October 7, 1896.

No attempt has been made as to scaling. It is the *wave patterns* and price levels that are of importance. As long as the 5-Wave pattern continues to unfold, it makes little difference if one wave is a bit above or below the previous wave. What is important is whether the price is going to move up or down over a period of time.

## The Grand Super Cycle Wave (1807 To 1984)

| Date | Value | Wave |
|---|---|---|
| Sept 1792 | $ 2.96 | |
| Dec 1818 | $ 11.03 | 1 |
| Jan 1820 | $ 9.59 | 2 |
| Oct 1827 | $ 12.33 | 3 |
| Jan 1829 | $ 10.48 | 4 |
| Aug 1835 | $ 23.48 | 5 |
| Mar 1842 | $ 5.74 | 6 |
| Jan 1853 | $ 21.13 | 1 |
| Oct 1857 | $ 7.99 | 2 |
| Feb 1874 | $ 35.68 | 3 |
| Jun 1877 | $ 22.08 | 4 |
| Jun 1889 | $ 49.99 | 5 |
| Apr 1897 | $ 38.67 | ext 6 |
| Jan 1906 | $ 103.00 | ext 7 |
| Nov 1907 | $ 53.00 | ext 8 |
| Nov 1916 | $ 110.15 | ext 9 |
| Dec 1917 | $ 65.95 | ext 10 |
| Sep 1929 | $ 381.17 | ext 11(5) (5) |
| Jul 1932 | $ 41.22 | 6 |
| Dec 1961 | $ 734.91 | 1 |
| Jun 1962 | $ 535.76 | 2 |
| Jan 1973 | $1051.70 | 3 |
| Dec 1974 | $ 577.60 | 4 |
| Currently in progress | | ...5 |

Super Cycle Wave 1

Super Cycle Wave 2

Insufficient Correction Wave 6

Super Cycle Wave 3

Super Cycle Wave 4

......Super Cycle Wave 5

## Super Cycle

| Date | Price | Primary Waves | Cycle-----Waves |
|------|-------|---------------|-----------------|
| Sep 1792 | $ 2.96 | | |
| Sep 1806 | $ 7.56 | 1 | |
| Oct 1807 | $ 3.57 | 2 | |
| Jun 1811 | $ 6.25 | 3 | |
| Mar 1813 | $ 4.43 | 4 | Wave 1 |
| Dec 1818 | $11.03 | 5 | |
| Jan 1820 | $ 9.59 | 6 | Wave 2 |
| Nov 1821 | $12.15 | 1 | |
| Sep 1822 | $11.19 | 2 | |
| Sep 1824 | $14.38 | 3 | |
| Oct 1826 | $11.33 | 4 | |
| | | | Wave 3 |
| Oct 1827 | $12.33 | 5 | |
| Jan 1829 | $10.48 | 6 | Wave 4 |
| Nov 1830 | $14.41 | 1 | |
| Nov 1831 | $11.74 | 2 | |
| May 1833 | $18.00 | 3 | |
| Feb 1834 | $13.31 | 4 | Wave 5 |
| Aug 1835 | $23.48 | 5 | |
| Mar 1842 | $ 5.74 | 6 | Wave 6 |

## Super Cycle

| Date | Price | Primary Waves | Cycle----Waves |
|---|---|---|---|
| Mar 1842 | $ 5.34 | | |
| May 1844 | $14.61 | 1 | |
| Sep 1845 | $12.00 | 2 | |
| Aug 1847 | $16.18 | 3 | Wave 1 |
| Nov 1848 | $12.26 | 4 | |
| Jan 1853 | $21.13 | 5 | |
| Oct 1857 | $ 7.99 | 6 | Wave 2 |
| Feb 1858 | $11.34 | 1 | |
| Jun 1859 | $ 8.33 | 2 | |
| Aug 1860 | $13.81 | 3 | |
| Aug 1861 | $11.27 | 4 | |
| Mar 1864 | $27.23 | 5 | Wave 3 |
| Mar 1865 | $21.07 | ext 6 | |
| Oct 1866 | $27.97 | ext 7 | |
| Apr 1867 | $23.96 | ext 8 | |
| Aug 1869 | $31.33 | ext 9 | |
| Mar 1870 | $25.53 | ext 10 | |
| Feb 1874 | $35.68 | ext 11 (5) | |
| Jun 1877 | $22.08 | 6 | Wave 4 |
| Jun 1881 | $36.24 | 1 | |
| Jun 1884 | $27.21 | 2 | |
| May 1887 | $38.60 | 3 | |
| Mar 1888 | $35.13 | 4 | |
| Jun 1889 | $49.99 | 5 | Wave 5 |
| Apr 1897 | $38.67 | 6 | Wave 6 |

135

## Super Cycle

| Date | Price | Primary Waves | Cycle--Waves |
|---|---|---|---|
| Apr 23, 1897 | $ 38.67 | | |
| Sep 5, 1899 | $ 77.61 | 1 | |
| Sep 24, 1900 | $ 52.96 | 2 | |
| Jun 17, 1901 | $ 78.26 | 3 | |
| Nov 9, 1903 | $ 42.15 | 4 | |
| Jan 19, 1906 | $103.00 | 5 | Wave 1 |
| Nov 15, 1907 | $ 53.00 | 6 | Wave 2 |
| Nov 19,1909 | $100.53 | 1 | |
| Sep 25, 1911 | $ 72.94 | 2 | |
| Sep 30, 1912 | $ 94.15 | 3 | |
| Feb 24, 1915 | $ 54.22 | 4 | |
| Nov 21, 1916 | $110.15 | 5 | Wave 3 |
| Dec 19, 1917 | $ 65.95 | 6 | Wave 4 |
| Nov 3, 1919 | $119.62 | 1 | |
| Aug 24, 1921 | $ 63.90 | 2 | |
| Feb 11, 1926 | $162.31 | 3 | |
| Mar 30, 1926 | $135.20 | 4 | |
| Sep 3, 1929 | $381.17 | 5 | Wave 5 |
| Jul 8, 1932 | $ 41.22 | 6 | Wave 6 |

## Super Cycle

| Date | Price | Primary Waves | Cycle--Waves |
|------|-------|---------------|--------------|
| Jul   8, 1932 | $   41.22 | | |
| Mar 10, 1937 | $ 194.40 | 1 | |
| Apr 28, 1942 | $   92.92 | 2 | |
| May 29, 1946 | $ 212.50 | 3 | |
| Jun 13, 1949 | $ 161.60 | 4 | |
| Apr   6, 1956 | $ 521.05 | 5 | |
| Oct 22, 1957 | $ 419.76 | ext 6 | |
| Jan   5, 1960 | $ 685.47 | ext 7 | |
| Oct 25, 1960 | $ 566.05 | ext 8 | |
| Dec 13, 1961 | $ 734.91 | ext 9 (5) | 1 |
| Jun 26, 1962 | $ 535.76 | 6 | 2 |
| Feb   9, 1966 | $ 995.15 | 1 | |
| Oct   7, 1966 | $ 744.32 | 2 | |
| Dec   3, 1968 | $ 985.21 | 3 | |
| May 26, 1970 | $ 631.16 | 4 | |
| Jan 11, 1973 | $1051.70 | 5 | 3 |
| Dec   6, 1974 | $ 577.60 | 6 | 4 |
| Sep 21, 1976 | $1014.79 | 1 | |
| Feb 28, 1978 | $ 742.12 | 2 | |
| Apr 27, 1981 | $1024.05 | 3 | |
| Aug 12, 1982 | $ 776.98 | 4 | |
| Jan   6, 1984 | $1286.64 | 5 | 5 |
| | | ext ????????? | |

Insufficient Loss For A Corrective Wave 6

**The Intermediate Waves Of**
**All Past Markets From 1897 to 1984**

**Bull Market**
**Intermediate Waves**

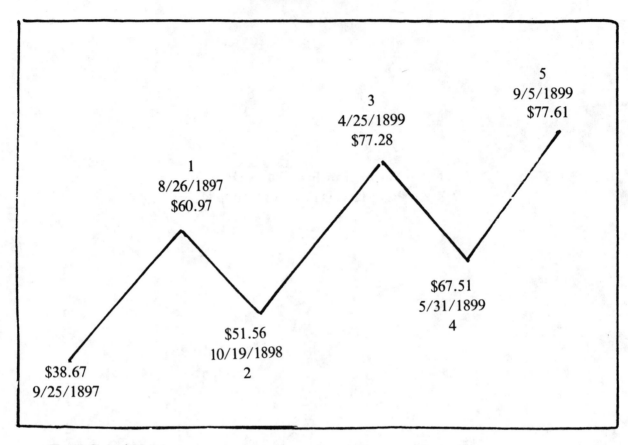

**Total Gain $38.94**

| Wave 1 | plus | $22.30 |
|--------|-------|--------|
| Wave 2 | minus | $ 9.41 |
| Wave 3 | plus | $25.72 |
| Wave 4 | minus | $ 9.77 |
| Wave 5 | plus | $10.10 |

**Bear Market**
**Intermediate Waves**

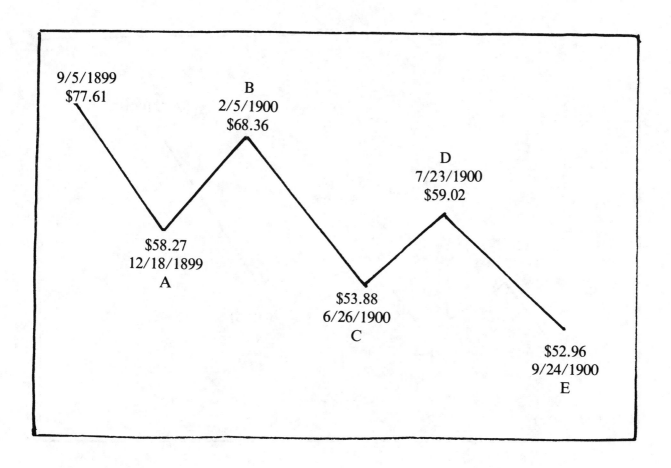

**Total Loss     $24.65**

| | | |
|---|---|---|
| Wave A | minus | $19.34 |
| Wave B | plus | $10.09 |
| Wave C | minus | $14.48 |
| Wave D | plus | $ 5.14 |
| Wave E | minus | $ 6.06 |

**Bull Market
Intermediate Waves**

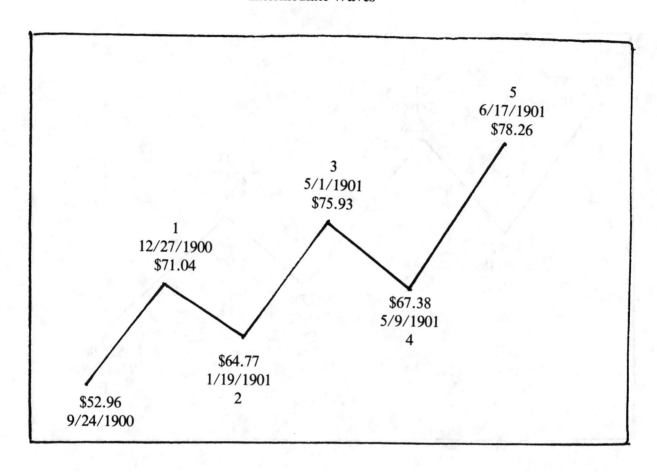

**Total Gain   $25.30**

Wave 1   plus    $18.08
Wave 2   minus   $ 6.27
Wave 3   plus    $11.16
Wave 4   minus   $ 8.55
Wave 5   plus    $10.88

**Bear Market**
**Intermediate Waves**

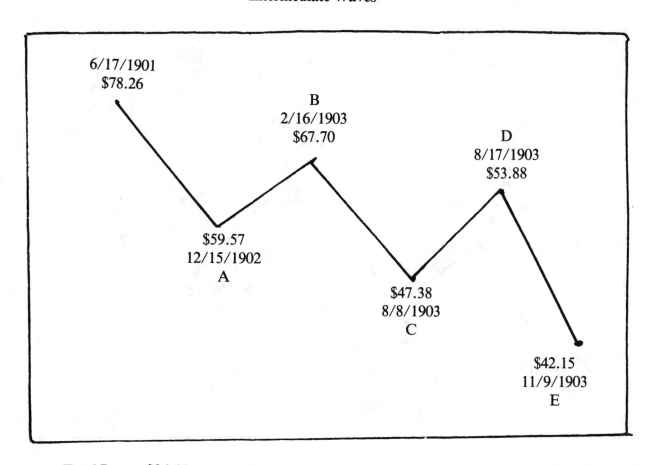

**Total Loss    $36.11**

| | | |
|---|---|---|
| Wave A | minus | $18.69 |
| Wave B | plus | $ 8.13 |
| Wave C | minus | $20.32 |
| Wave D | plus | $ 6.50 |
| Wave E | minus | $11.73 |

**Bull Market**
**Intermediate Waves**

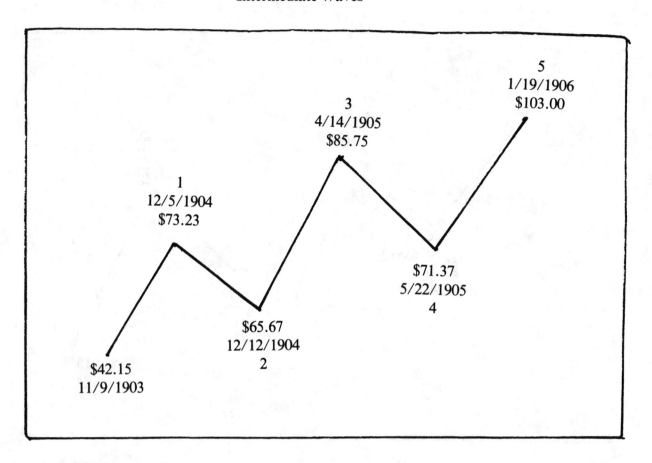

**Total Gain    $60.85**

| | | |
|---|---|---|
| Wave 1 | plus | $31.08 |
| Wave 2 | minus | $ 7.56 |
| Wave 3 | plus | $20.08 |
| Wave 4 | minus | $14.38 |
| Wave 5 | plus | $31.63 |

**Bear Market**
**Intermediate Waves**

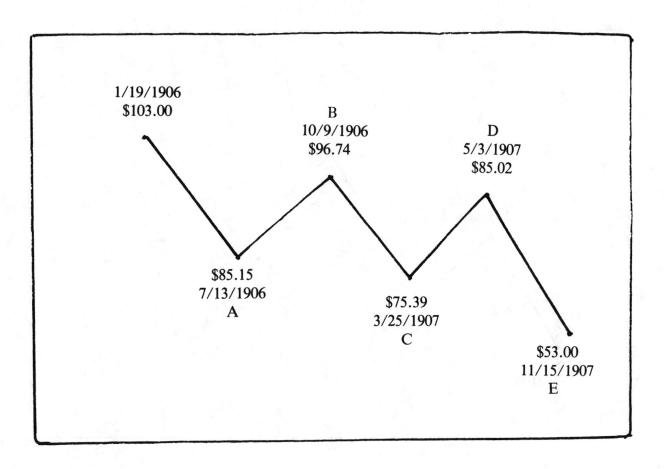

1/19/1906
$103.00

B
10/9/1906
$96.74

D
5/3/1907
$85.02

$85.15
7/13/1906
A

$75.39
3/25/1907
C

$53.00
11/15/1907
E

**Total Loss    $50.00**

Wave A   minus    $17.83
Wave B   plus     $11.57
Wave C   minus    $21.35
Wave D   plus     $ 9.63
Wave E   minus    $32.02

## Bull Market
## Intermediate Waves

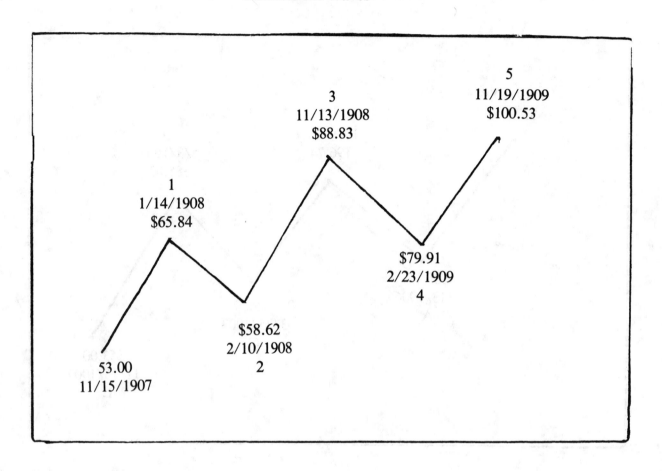

**Total Gain    $47.53**

| | | |
|---|---|---|
| Wave 1 | plus | $12.84 |
| Wave 2 | minus | $ 7.22 |
| Wave 3 | plus | $30.21 |
| Wave 4 | minus | $ 8.92 |
| Wave 5 | plus | $20.62 |

**Bear Market**
**Intermediate Waves**

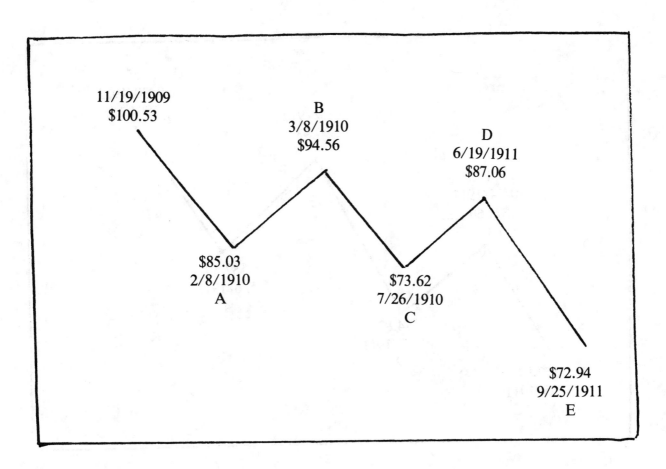

**Total Loss     $27.59**

| Wave A | minus | $15.50 |
| Wave B | plus  | $ 9.53 |
| Wave C | minus | $20.94 |
| Wave D | plus  | $13.44 |
| Wave E | minus | $14.12 |

## Bull Market
## Intermediate Waves

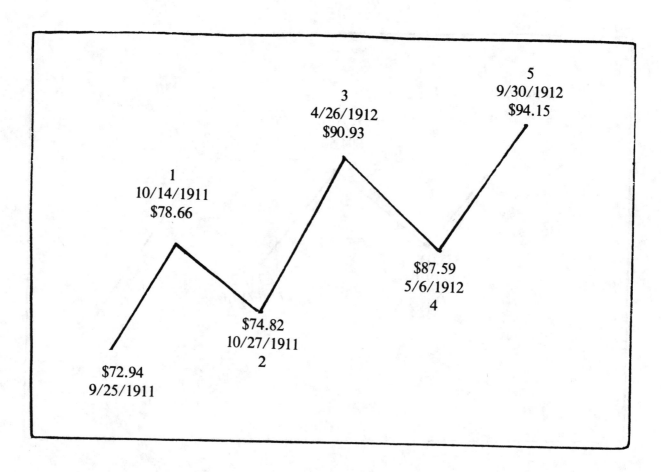

**Total Gain $21.21**

| Wave 1 | plus | $ 5.72 |
|--------|-------|--------|
| Wave 2 | minus | $ 3.84 |
| Wave 3 | plus | $16.11 |
| Wave 4 | minus | $ 3.34 |
| Wave 5 | plus | $ 6.56 |

**Bear Market**
**Intermediate Waves**

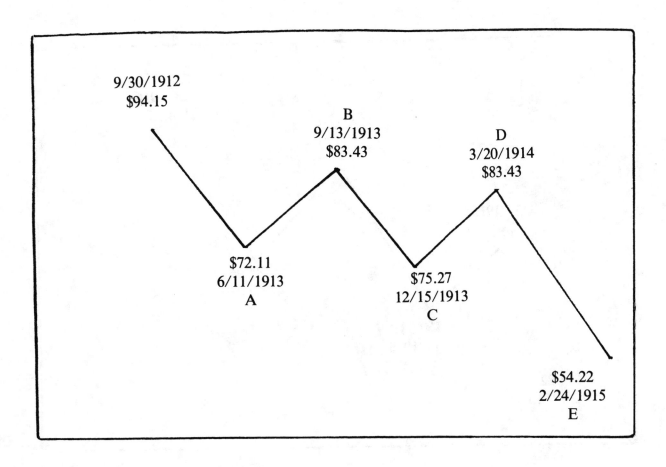

**Total Loss      $39.93**

| | | |
|---|---|---|
| Wave A | minus | $22.04 |
| Wave B | plus | $11.32 |
| Wave C | minus | $ 8.16 |
| Wave D | plus | $ 8.16 |
| Wave E | minus | $29.21 |

**Bull Market**
**Intermediate Waves**

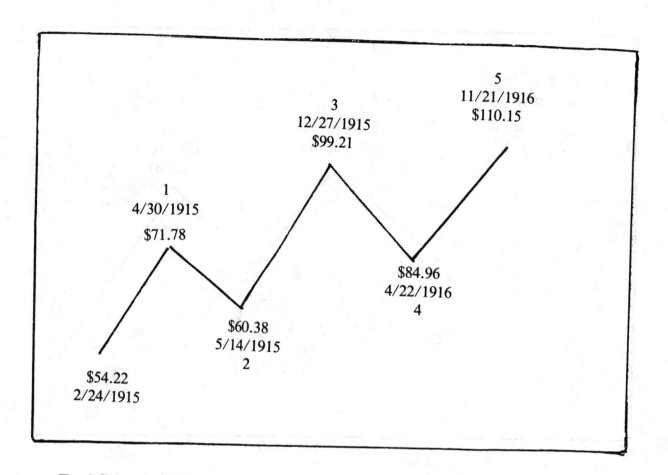

**Total Gain    $55.93**

| | | |
|---|---|---|
| Wave 1 | plus | $17.56 |
| Wave 2 | minus | $11.40 |
| Wave 3 | plus | $38.83 |
| Wave 4 | minus | $14.25 |
| Wave 5 | plus | $25.19 |

**Bear Market**
**Intermediate Waves**

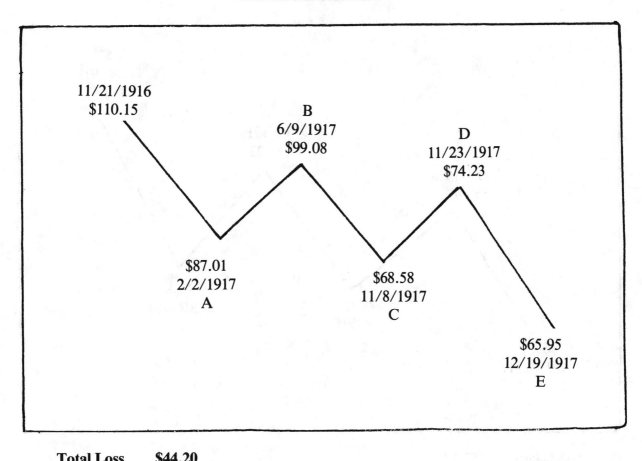

11/21/1916
$110.15

B
6/9/1917
$99.08

D
11/23/1917
$74.23

$87.01
2/2/1917
A

$68.58
11/8/1917
C

$65.95
12/19/1917
E

**Total Loss      $44.20**

| Wave A | minus | $23.14 |
|--------|-------|--------|
| Wave B | plus  | $12.07 |
| Wave C | minus | $30.50 |
| Wave D | plus  | $ 5.65 |
| Wave E | minus | $ 8.28 |

**Bull Market
Intermediate Waves**

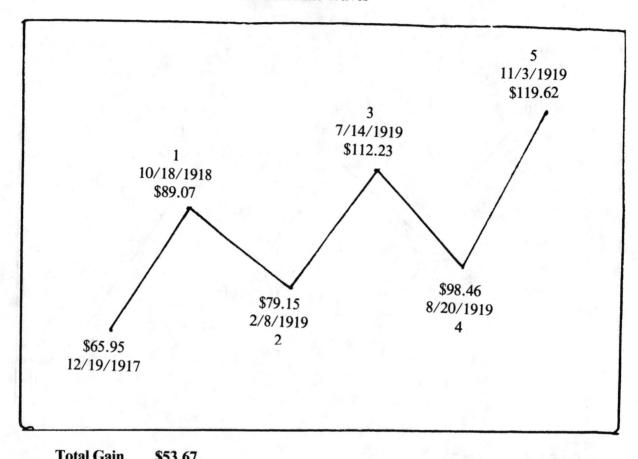

**Total Gain       $53.67**

| Wave 1 | plus  | $23.12 |
|--------|-------|--------|
| Wave 2 | minus | $ 9.92 |
| Wave 3 | plus  | $33.08 |
| Wave 4 | minus | $13.77 |
| Wave 5 | plus  | $21.16 |

**Bear Market**
**Intermediate Waves**

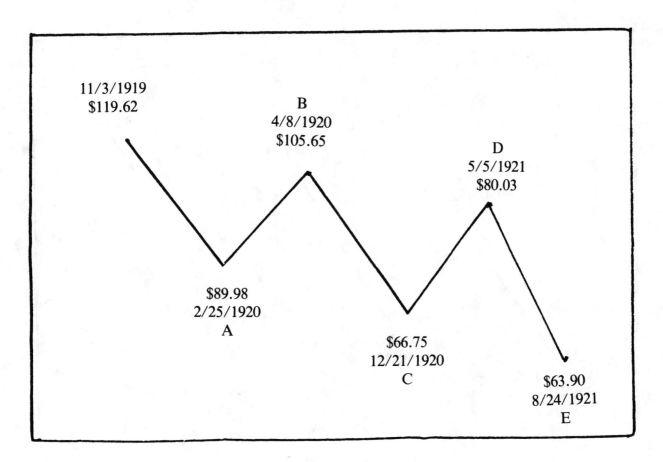

11/3/1919
$119.62

B
4/8/1920
$105.65

D
5/5/1921
$80.03

$89.98
2/25/1920
A

$66.75
12/21/1920
C

$63.90
8/24/1921
E

**Total Loss** **$55.72**

| | | |
|---|---|---|
| Wave A | minus | $29.64 |
| Wave B | plus | $15.67 |
| Wave C | minus | $38.90 |
| Wave D | plus | $13.28 |
| Wave E | minus | $16.13 |

**Bull Market**
**Intermediate Waves**

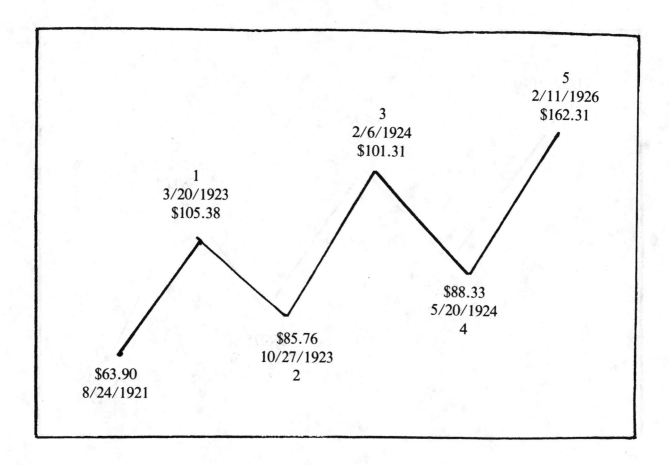

**Total Gain        $98.41**

| Wave 1 | plus | $41.48 |
|--------|-------|--------|
| Wave 2 | minus | $19.62 |
| Wave 3 | plus | $15.55 |
| Wave 4 | minus | $12.98 |
| Wave 5 | plus | $73.98 |

**Bear Market**
**Intermediate Waves**

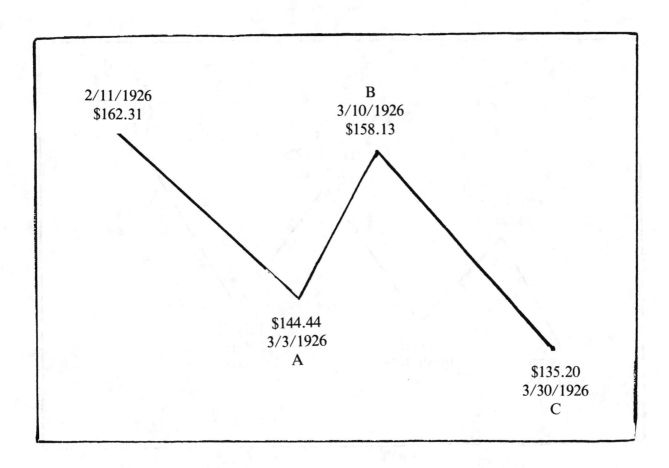

2/11/1926
$162.31

B
3/10/1926
$158.13

$144.44
3/3/1926
A

$135.20
3/30/1926
C

**Total Loss      $27.11**

Wave A   minus     $17.87
Wave B   plus      $ 8.69
Wave C   minus     $17.93

**Bull Market**
**Intermediate Waves**

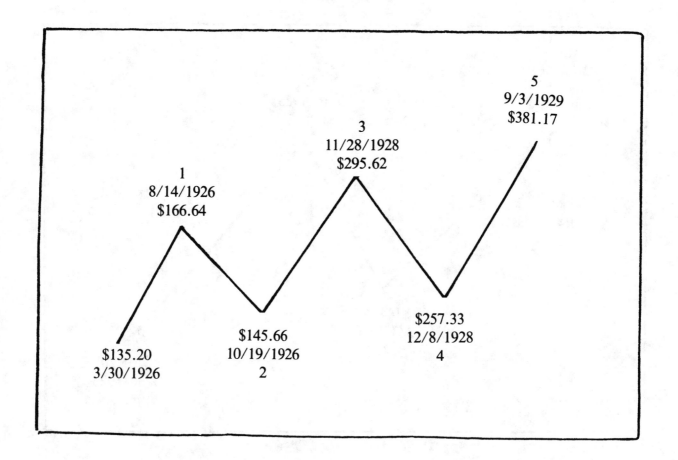

**Total Gain      $245.97**

| Wave 1 | plus  | $ 31.44  |
|--------|-------|----------|
| Wave 2 | minus | $ 20.98  |
| Wave 3 | plus  | $149.96  |
| Wave 4 | minus | $ 38.29  |
| Wave 5 | plus  | $123.84  |

**Bear Market**
**Intermediate Waves**

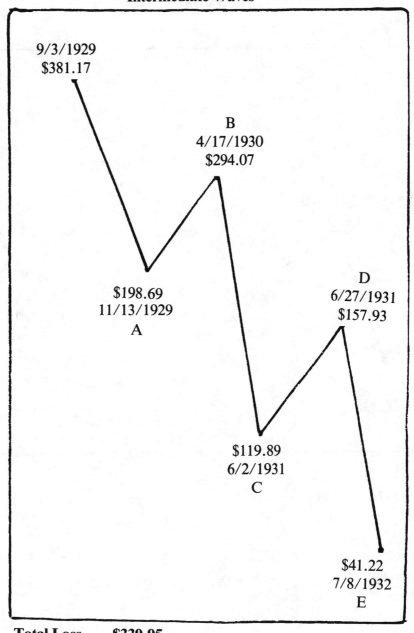

**Total Loss      $339.95**

| Wave A | minus | $182.48 |
|--------|-------|---------|
| Wave B | plus | $ 95.38 |
| Wave C | minus | $174.18 |
| Wave D | plus | $ 38.04 |
| Wave E | minus | $116.71 |

157

**Bull Market**
**Intermediate Waves**

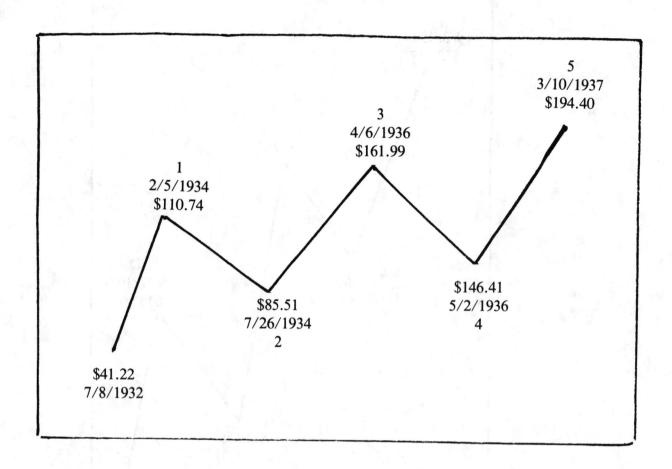

**Total Gain        $153.18**

| | | |
|---|---|---|
| Wave 1 | plus | $69.52 |
| Wave 2 | minus | $25.23 |
| Wave 3 | plus | $76.48 |
| Wave 4 | minus | $15.58 |
| Wave 5 | plus | $47.99 |

**Bear Market**
**Intermediate Waves**

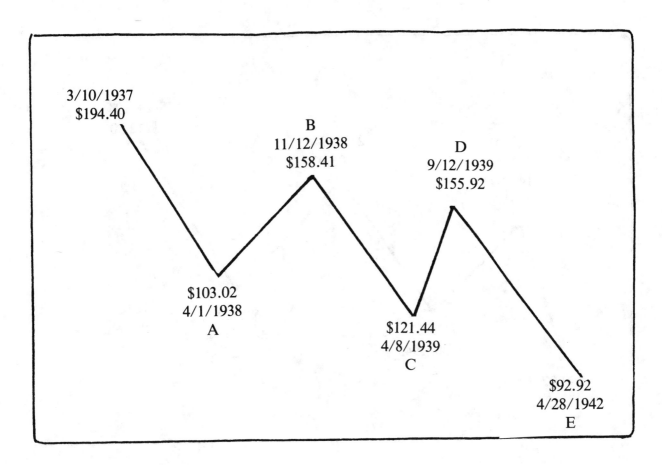

3/10/1937
$194.40

B
11/12/1938
$158.41

D
9/12/1939
$155.92

$103.02
4/1/1938
A

$121.44
4/8/1939
C

$92.92
4/28/1942
E

**Total Loss**    **$101.48**

Wave A   minus   $91.38
Wave B   plus    $55.39
Wave C   minus   $36.97
Wave D   plus    $34.48
Wave E   minus   $63.00

**Bull Market**
**Intermediate Waves**

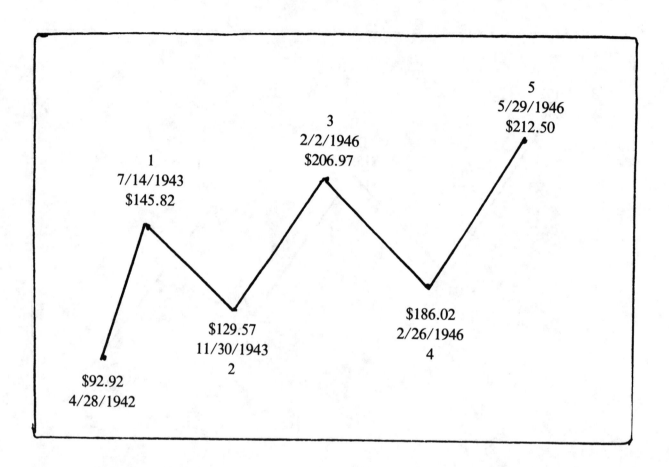

**Total Gain        $119.58**

| | | |
|---|---|---|
| Wave 1 | plus | $52.90 |
| Wave 2 | minus | $16.25 |
| Wave 3 | plus | $77.40 |
| Wave 4 | minus | $20.95 |
| Wave 5 | plus | $26.48 |

**Bear Market
Intermediate Waves**

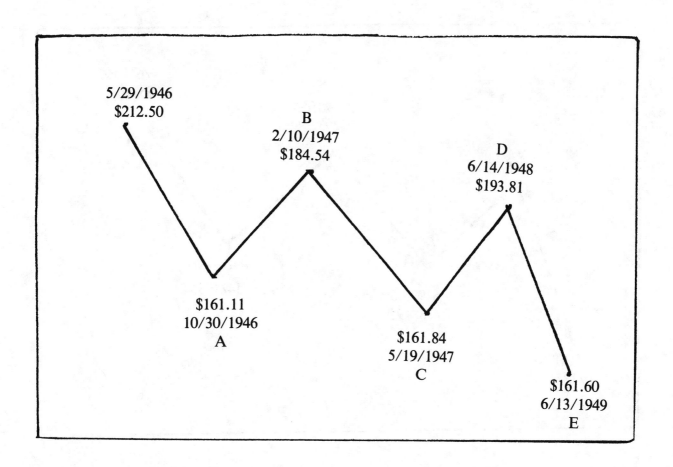

**Total Loss        $51.40**

| | | |
|---|---|---|
| Wave A | minus | $51.39 |
| Wave B | plus | $23.42 |
| Wave C | minus | $22.70 |
| Wave D | plus | $31.97 |
| Wave E | minus | $32.21 |

**Bull Market
Intermediate Waves**

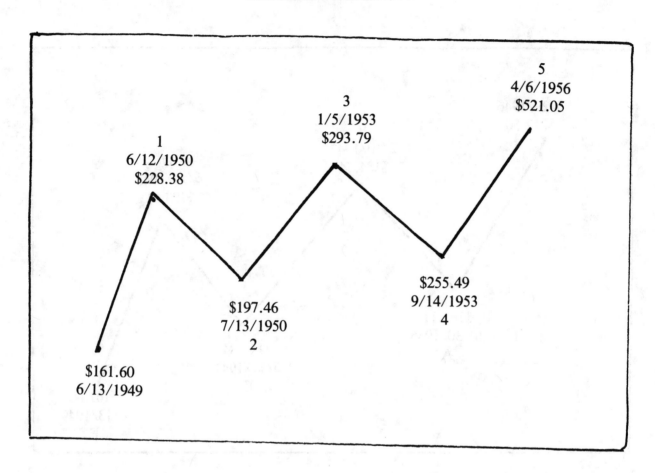

**Total Gain        $350.95**

| | | |
|---|---|---|
| Wave 1 | plus | $ 66.78 |
| Wave 2 | minus | $ 30.92 |
| Wave 3 | plus | $ 96.33 |
| Wave 4 | minus | $ 38.30 |
| Wave 5 | plus | $265.56 |

**Bear Market**
**Intermediate Waves**

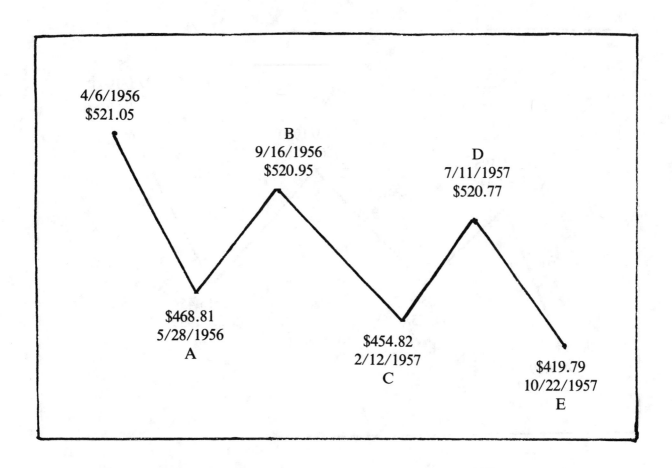

**Total Loss      $101.26**

| | | |
|---|---|---|
| Wave A | minus | $ 52.24 |
| Wave B | plus | $ 52.14 |
| Wave C | minus | $ 66.13 |
| Wave D | plus | $ 65.95 |
| Wave E | minus | $100.98 |

163

**Bull Market**
**Intermediate Waves**

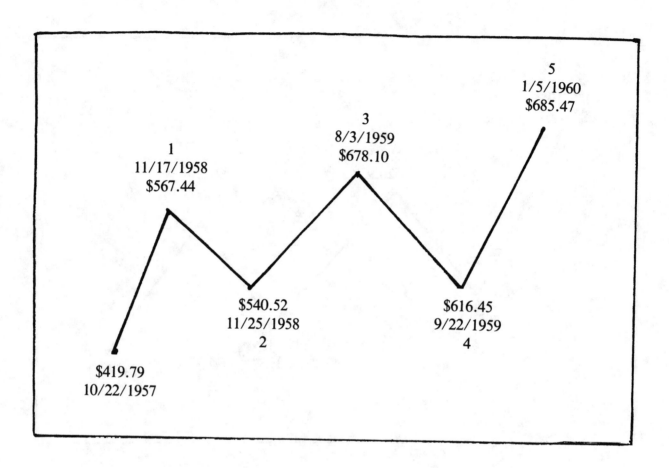

**Total Gain      $265.68**

| | | |
|---|---|---|
| Wave 1 | plus | $147.65 |
| Wave 2 | minus | $ 26.92 |
| Wave 3 | plus | $137.58 |
| Wave 4 | minus | $ 61.65 |
| Wave 5 | plus | $ 69.02 |

**Bear Market**
**Intermediate Waves**

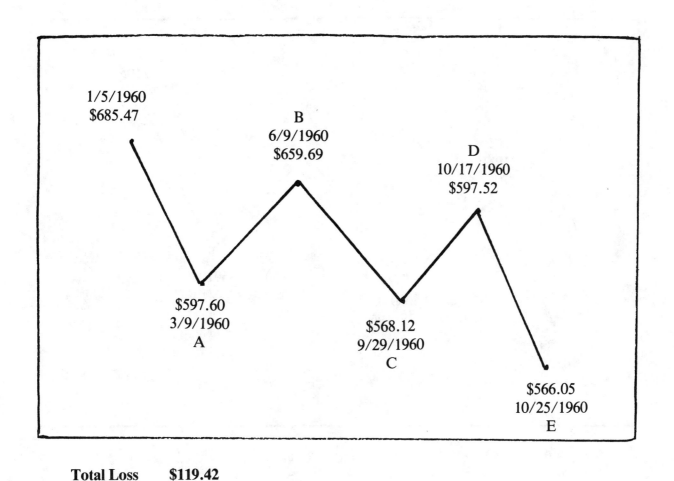

1/5/1960
$685.47

B
6/9/1960
$659.69

D
10/17/1960
$597.52

$597.60
3/9/1960
A

$568.12
9/29/1960
C

$566.05
10/25/1960
E

**Total Loss       $119.42**

| Wave A | minus | $87.87 |
| Wave B | plus | $62.09 |
| Wave C | minus | $91.57 |
| Wave D | plus | $29.40 |
| Wave E | minus | $31.47 |

**Bull Market**
**Intermediate Waves**

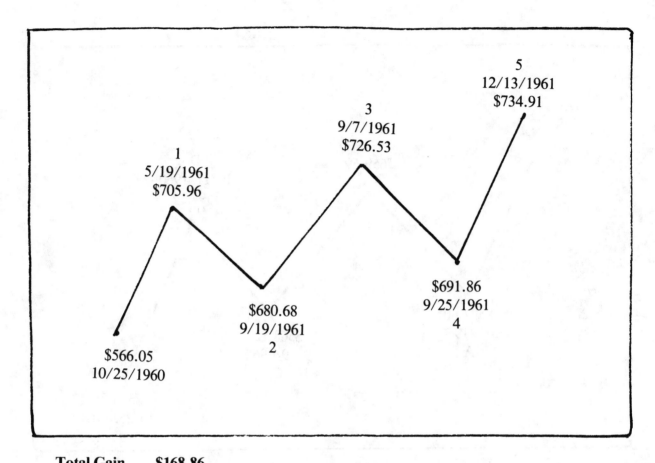

| | | |
|---|---|---|
| **Total Gain** | | **$168.86** |
| Wave 1 | plus | $139.91 |
| Wave 2 | minus | $ 25.28 |
| Wave 3 | plus | $ 45.85 |
| Wave 4 | minus | $ 34.67 |
| Wave 5 | plus | $ 43.05 |

**Bear Market**
**Intermediate Waves**

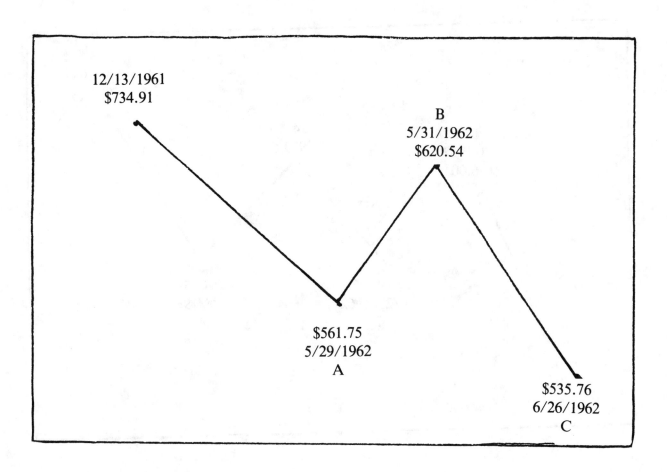

12/13/1961
$734.91

B
5/31/1962
$620.54

$561.75
5/29/1962
A

$535.76
6/26/1962
C

**Total Loss**     **$199.15**

| | | |
|---|---|---|
| Wave A | minus | $173.16 |
| Wave B | plus | $ 58.79 |
| Wave C | minus | $ 84.78 |

**Bull Market**
**Intermediate Waves**

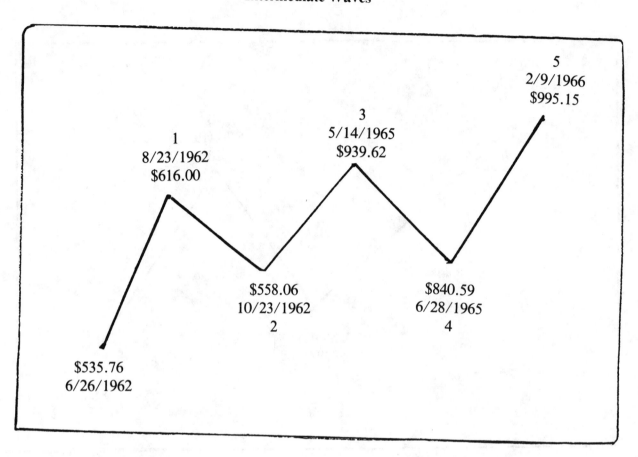

**Total Gain $459.39**

| | | |
|---|---|---|
| Wave 1 | plus | $ 80.24 |
| Wave 2 | minus | $ 57.94 |
| Wave 3 | plus | $381.56 |
| Wave 4 | minus | $ 99.03 |
| Wave 5 | plus | $154.56 |

**Bear Market**
**Intermediate Waves**

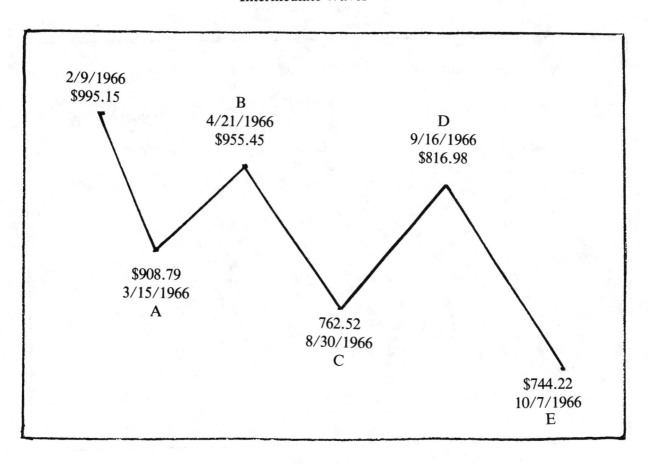

2/9/1966
$995.15

B
4/21/1966
$955.45

D
9/16/1966
$816.98

$908.79
3/15/1966
A

762.52
8/30/1966
C

$744.22
10/7/1966
E

**Total Loss      $250.93**

| | | |
|---|---|---|
| Wave A | minus | $ 86.36 |
| Wave B | plus | $ 46.66 |
| Wave C | minus | $192.93 |
| Wave D | plus | $ 54.46 |
| Wave E | minus | $ 72.76 |

## Bull Market
## Intermediate Waves

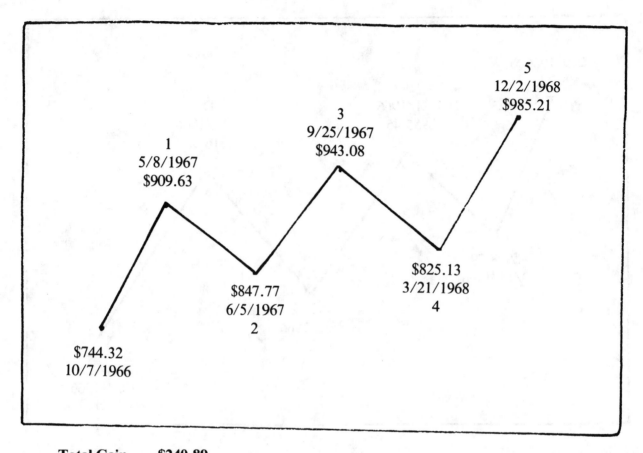

**Total Gain       $240.89**

| Wave 1 | plus  | $165.31 |
|--------|-------|---------|
| Wave 2 | minus | $ 61.86 |
| Wave 3 | plus  | $ 95.31 |
| Wave 4 | minus | $117.95 |
| Wave 5 | plus  | $160.08 |

**Bear Market**
**Intermediate Waves**

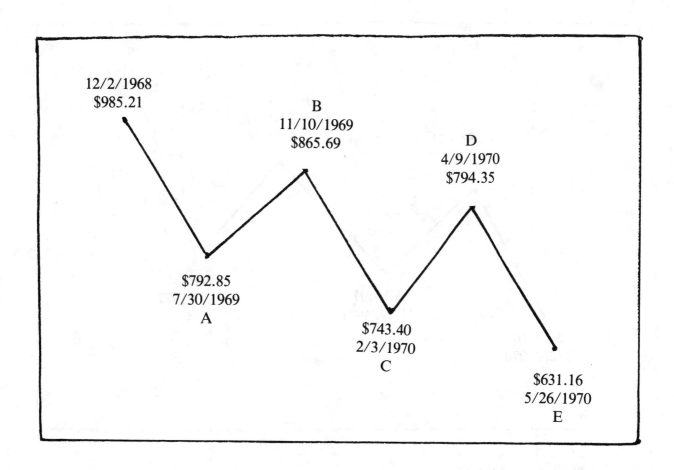

12/2/1968
$985.21

B
11/10/1969
$865.69

D
4/9/1970
$794.35

$792.85
7/30/1969
A

$743.40
2/3/1970
C

$631.16
5/26/1970
E

**Total Loss      $354.05**

| Wave A | minus | $192.36 |
|--------|-------|---------|
| Wave B | plus  | $ 72.84 |
| Wave C | minus | $122.29 |
| Wave D | plus  | $ 50.95 |
| Wave E | minus | $163.19 |

171

**Bull Market**
**Intermediate Waves**

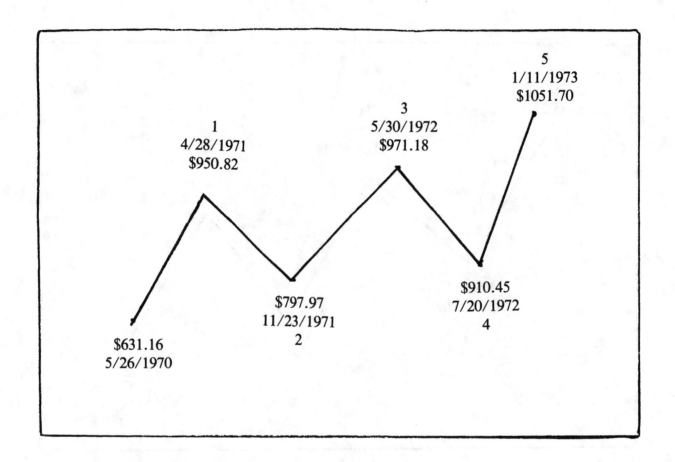

**Total Gain       $384.54**

| | | |
|---|---|---|
| Wave 1 | plus | $319.66 |
| Wave 2 | minus | $152.85 |
| Wave 3 | plus | $173.21 |
| Wave 4 | minus | $ 60.73 |
| Wave 5 | plus | $141.25 |

**Bear Market
Intermediate Waves**

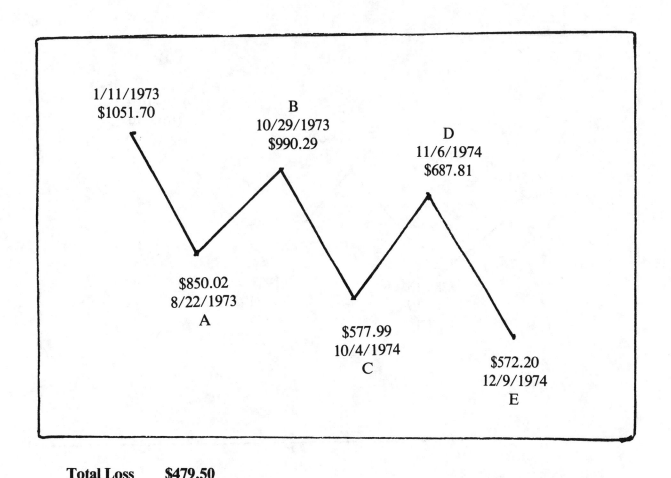

1/11/1973
$1051.70

B
10/29/1973
$990.29

D
11/6/1974
$687.81

$850.02
8/22/1973
A

$577.99
10/4/1974
C

$572.20
12/9/1974
E

**Total Loss      $479.50**

Wave A    minus      $201.68
Wave B    plus       $140.27
Wave C    minus      $412.30
Wave D    plus       $109.82
Wave E    minus      $115.61

**Bull Market**
**Intermediate Waves**

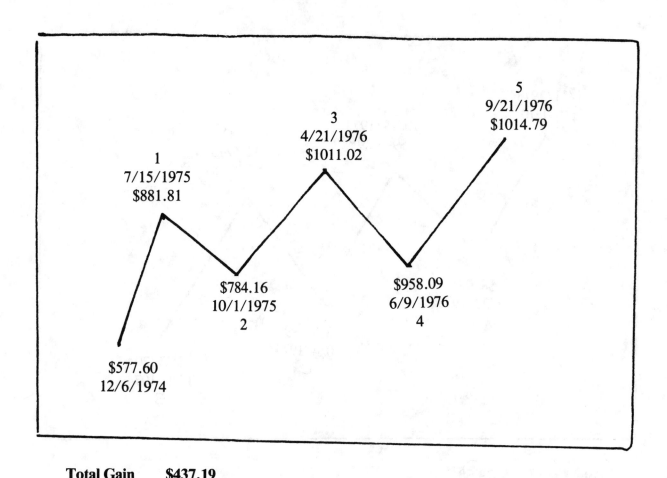

**Total Gain      $437.19**

| | | |
|---|---|---|
| Wave 1 | plus | $304.21 |
| Wave 2 | minus | $ 67.65 |
| Wave 3 | plus | $226.86 |
| Wave 4 | minus | $ 52.93 |
| Wave 5 | plus | $ 56.70 |

174

**Bear Market**
**Intermediate Waves**

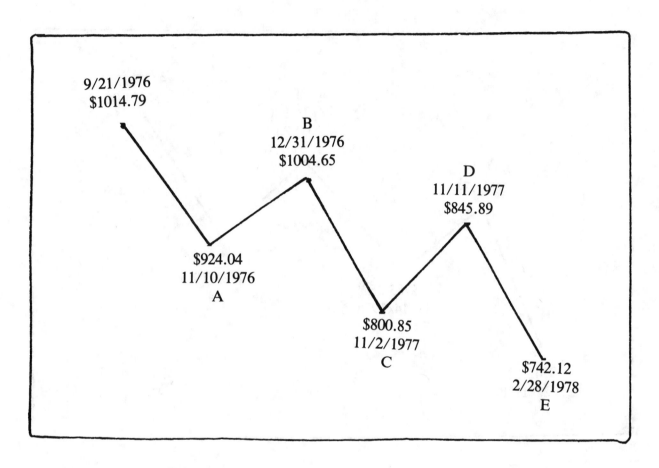

**Total Loss      $272.67**

| Wave A | minus | $ 90.75 |
|--------|-------|---------|
| Wave B | plus | $ 80.61 |
| Wave C | minus | $203.80 |
| Wave D | plus | $ 45.04 |
| Wave E | minus | $103.77 |

**Bull Market**
**Intermediate Waves**

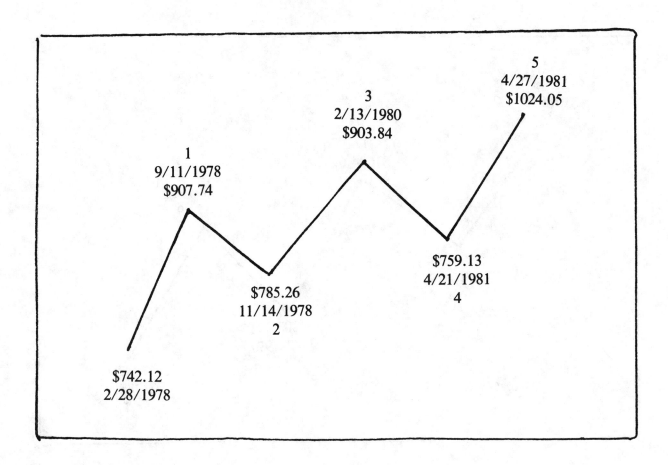

**Total Gain          $281.93**

| | | |
|---|---|---|
| Wave 1 | plus | $165.62 |
| Wave 2 | minus | $122.48 |
| Wave 3 | plus | $118.58 |
| Wave 4 | minus | $144.71 |
| Wave 5 | plus | $264.92 |

**Bear Market**
**Intermediate Waves**

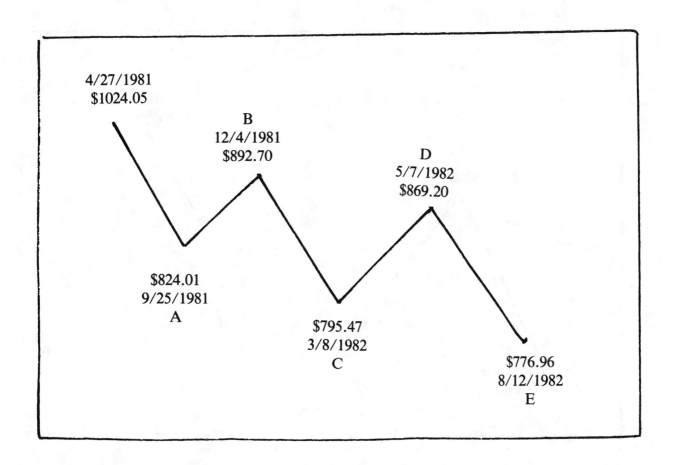

4/27/1981
$1024.05

B
12/4/1981
$892.70

D
5/7/1982
$869.20

$824.01
9/25/1981
A

$795.47
3/8/1982
C

$776.96
8/12/1982
E

**Total Loss      $247.09**

| | | |
|---|---|---|
| Wave A | minus | $200.04 |
| Wave B | plus | $ 68.69 |
| Wave C | minus | $ 97.23 |
| Wave D | plus | $ 73.73 |
| Wave E | minus | $ 92.24 |

## Bear Market
## Intermediate Waves

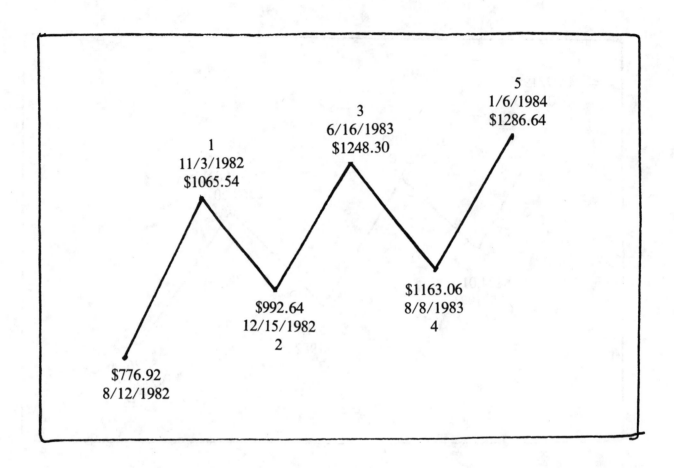

**Total Gain        $509.72**

| | | |
|---|---|---|
| Wave 1 | plus | $288.58 |
| Wave 2 | minus | $ 72.90 |
| Wave 3 | plus | $256.30 |
| Wave 4 | minus | $ 85.27 |
| Wave 5 | plus | $123.58 |

# A Look At The Present
## And
## A "Clue" For The Future

**Bear Market**
**1/6/1984 to 7/24/1984**

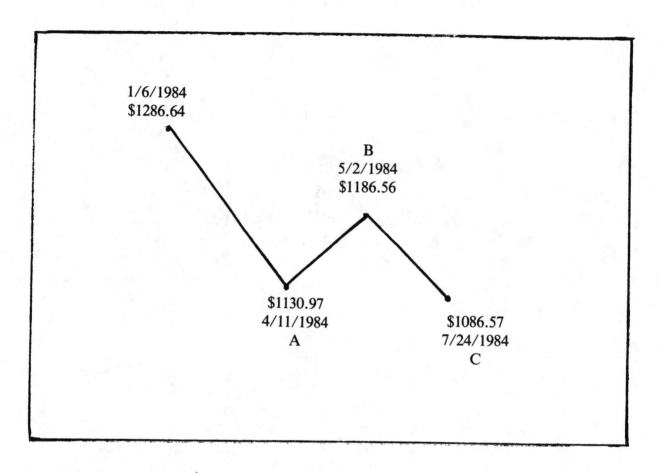

**Total Loss     $200.07**

| Wave A | minus | $155.67 |
|--------|-------|---------|
| Wave B | plus  | $ 55.59 |
| Wave C | minus | $ 99.99 |

## Bear Market
## Chart 1 - Minor Waves

| Date | Close New Highs | Close New Lows | Direction Reversal Price $24.00 | Minor Wave Count | Intermediate Wave Count |
|------|-----------------|----------------|----------------------------------|------------------|--------------------------|
| 1- 6-84 | 1287. | | 1263. | | Dow High |
| 1-20-84 | | 1259. | 1283. | | |
| 1-26-84 | | 1230. | 1254. | | |
| 2- 1-84 | | 1212. | 1236. | | |
| 2- 3-84 | | 1197. | 1221. | | |
| 2- 6-84 | | 1174. | 1198. | | |
| 2- 9-84 | | 1153. | 1177. | | |
| 2-13-84 | | 1150. | 1174. | | |
| 2-17-84 | | 1149. | 1173. | | |
| 2-21-84 | | 1139. | 1163. | | |
| 2-22-84 | | 1134. | 1158. | 1 | |
| 2-24-84 | 1165. | | 1141. | | |
| 2-27-84 | 1180. | | 1156. | 2 | |
| 2-29-84 | | 1155. | 1179. | | |
| 3- 7-84 | | 1144. | 1168. | | |
| 3 9-84 | | 1140. | 1164. | 3 | |
| 3-13-84 | 1165. | | 1141. | | |
| 3-16-84 | 1184. | | 1160. | 4 | |
| 3-22-84 | | 1156. | 1180. | | |
| 3-23-84 | | 1155. | 1179. | | |
| 3-26-84 | | 1153. | 1177. | | |
| 4- 4-84 | | 1149. | 1173. | | |
| 4- 5-84 | | 1131. | 1155. | | |
| 4-11-84 | | 1131. | 1155. | 5 | A |
| 4-12-84 | 1157. | | 1133. | | |
| 4-17-84 | 1165. | | 1141. | | |
| 4-26-84 | 1175. | | 1151. | | |
| 5- 2-84 | 1187. | | 1163. | 6 | B |
| 5-11-84 | | 1157. | 1181. | | |
| 5-15-84 | | 1151. | 1175. | | |
| 5-17-84 | | 1142. | 1166. | | |
| 5-23-84 | | 1114. | 1138. | | |
| 5-24-84 | | 1103. | 1127. | | |
| 5-29-84 | | 1101. | 1125. | 1 | |
| 6- 4-84 | 1132. | | 1108. | | |
| 6- 6-84 | 1134. | | 1110. | 2 | |
| 6-14-84 | | 1098. | 1122. | | |
| 6-15-84 | | 1086. | 1110. | 3 | |
| 6-18-84 | 1110. | | 1086. | | |
| 6-20-84 | 1132. | | 1108. | | |
| 7- 3-84 | 1134. | | 1110. | 4 | |

181

## Bear Market (Cont'd)
## Chart 1 - Minor Waves

| Date | Close New Highs | Close New Lows | Direction Reversal Price $24.00 | Minor Wave Count | Intermediate Wave Count |
|------|------|------|------|------|------|
| 7-11-84 | | 1109. | 1133. | | |
| 7-12-84 | | 1105. | 1129. | | |
| 7-20-84 | | 1101. | 1125. | | |
| 7-24-84 | | 1087. | 1111. | 5 | C |

By August 21, the market had risen 153.00 points. This was certainly not a corrective Wave D in a Bear Market, but the start of a new Bull move upwards.

From Page 170, we can see that the last Bull Market was the 5th Wave of a 5th Wave in a Super Cycle. A "crash" wave should have followed the Bull Market peak of 1984. This Bear move just is *not* of the magnitude to qualify as a "crash." In fact, it isn't even as strong as the previous two Bear Markets of the Cycle, which began Dec 6, 1974. Therefore, it can only be termed as an *extension*, and the final peak of this Super Cycle is yet to be reached!

It is extremely *important* at this time to pay close attention to our wave patterns and our charts, for the top of this Super Cycle is very near.

As of this moment, we have entered the final moves upward. Bull Move Chart 1 follows, in order to keep this book as up to the minute as possible.

## Bull Market
## 7-24-84 to 8-24-87

| Date | Close New Highs | Close New Lows | Direction Reversal Price | Minor Wave Count $38.00 | Intermediate Wave Count |
|---|---|---|---|---|---|
| 7-24-84 | | 1087. | 1111. | Dow Bottom | |
| 7-27-84 | 1115. | | 1077. | | |
| 8- 7-84 | 1205. | | 1167. | | |
| 8- 9-84 | 1224. | | 1186. | | |
| 8-21-84 | 1240. | | 1202. | 1 | |
| 9-10-84 | | 1202. | 1240. | | |
| 9-11-84 | | 1198. | 1236. | 2 | |
| 9-14-84 | 1238. | | 1200. | 3 | |
| 10- 1-84 | | 1199. | 1237. | | |
| 10- 2-84 | | 1191. | 1229. | | |
| 10- 3-84 | | 1183. | 1221. | | |
| 10- 9-84 | | 1175. | 1213. | 4 | |
| 10-18-84 | 1225. | | 1187. | | |
| 10-19-84 | 1226. | | 1188. | | |
| 11- 5-84 | 1229. | | 1191. | | |
| 11- 6-84 | 1244. | | 1206. | 5 | 1 |
| 11-15-84 | | 1206. | 1244. | | |
| 11-16-84 | | 1188. | 1226. | | |
| 11-19-84 | | 1185. | 1223. | (see Minute | |
| 12- 3-84 | | 1182. | 1220. | Wave Chart) | |
| 12- 5-84 | | 1172. | 1210. | | |
| 12- 6-84 | | 1170. | 1208. | | |
| 12- 7-84 | | 1163. | 1201. | A,B, C | 2 |
| 12-18-84 | 1212. | | 1174. | | |
| 1-10-85 | 1224. | | 1186. | | |
| 1-14-85 | 1235. | | 1197. | | |
| 1-21-85 | 1261. | | 1223. | | |
| 1-23-85 | 1275. | | 1237. | | |
| 1-25-85 | 1276. | | 1238. | | |
| 1-28-85 | 1278. | | 1240. | | |
| 1-29-85 | 1293. | | 1255. | | |
| 2-13-85 | 1298. | | 1260. | | |
| 3- 1-85 | 1299. | | 1261. | 1 | |
| 3-14-85 | | 1260. | 1298. | | |
| 3-15-85 | | 1247. | 1285. | 2 | |
| 4-25-85 | 1285. | | 1247. | 3 | |
| 5- 1-85 | | 1242. | | 4 | |
| 5-17-85 | 1285. | | 1280. | | |
| 5-20-85 | 1305. | | 1267. | | |
| 5-21-85 | 1310. | | 1272. | | |
| 5-31-85 | 1315. | | 1277. | | |
| 6- 5-85 | 1321. | | 1283. | | |
| 6- 6-85 | 1327. | | 1289. | | |
| 6-27-85 | 1332. | | 1294. | | |
| 5-28-85 | 1335. | | 1297. | | |
| 7- 1-85 | 1337. | | 1299. | | |
| 7-11-85 | 1338. | | 1300. | | |

## Bull Market (Cont'd)
## 7-24-84 to 8-24-87

| Date | Close New Highs | Close New Lows | Direction Reversal Price | Minor Wave Count $38.00 | Intermediate Wave Count |
|---|---|---|---|---|---|
| 7-12-85 | 1339. | | 1301. | | |
| 7-16-85 | 1348. | | 1310. | | |
| 7-17-85 | 1358. | | 1320. | | |
| 7-19-85 | 1360. | | 1322. | 5 | 3 |
| 8- 9-85 | | 1321. | 1359. | | |
| 8-12-85 | | 1314. | 1352. | (see Minute | |
| 8-16-85 | | 1313. | 1351. | Wave Chart) | |
| 8-19-85 | | 1312. | 1350. | | |
| 9-13-85 | | 1308. | 1346. | | |
| 9-17-85 | | 1298. | 1336. | A,B,C | 4 |
| 10- 1-85 | 1341. | | 1303. | | |
| 10-14-85 | 1355. | | 1317. | | |
| 10-16-85 | 1369. | | 1331. | | |
| 10-30-85 | 1376. | | 1338. | | |
| 11- 1-85 | 1390. | | 1352. | | |
| 11- 5-85 | 1397. | | 1359. | | |
| 11- 6-85 | 1403. | | 1365. | | |
| 11- 8-85 | 1404. | | 1366. | | |
| 11-11-85 | 1432. | | 1394. | | |
| 11-12-85 | 1434. | | 1396. | | |
| 11-14-85 | 1439. | | 1401. | | |
| 11-18-85 | 1440. | | 1402. | | |
| 11-21-85 | 1462. | | 1424. | | |
| 11-22-85 | 1464. | | 1426. | | |
| 11-27-85 | 1476. | | 1438. | | |
| 12- 4-85 | 1484. | | 1446. | | |
| 12- 9-85 | 1497. | | 1459. | | |
| 12-10-85 | 1499. | | 1461. | | |
| 12-11-85 | 1512. | | 1474. | | |
| 12-13-85 | 1535. | | 1497. | | |
| 12-16-85 | 1553. | | 1515. | | |
| 1- 7-86 | 1566. | | 1528. | 1 | |
| 1- 8-86 | | 1528. | 1565. | | |
| 1- 9-86 | | 1518. | 1556. | (see Minute | |
| 1-10-86 | | 1514. | 1552. | Wave Chart) | |
| 1-22-86 | | 1502. | 1540. | 2 | |
| 1-28-86 | 1557. | | 1519. | | |
| 1-29-86 | 1559. | | 1521. | | |
| 1-31-86 | 1571. | | 1533. | | |
| 2- 3-86 | 1594. | | 1556. | | |
| 2- 6-86 | 1601. | | 1563. | | |
| 2- 7-86 | 1613. | | 1575. | | |

## Minute Wave Chart For Intermediate Wave 2
### Showing The A,B, and C Reactions. *At Value* $24.00 (.236)

| Date | Close New Highs | Close New Lows | Direction Reversal Price | Minor Wave Count | Intermediate Wave Count |
|------|-----------------|----------------|--------------------------|------------------|-------------------------|
| 11- 6-84 | 1244. | | 1220. | 5 | 1 |
| 11- 9-84 | | 1219. | 1243. | | |
| 11-13-84 | | 1207. | 1231. | | |
| 11-19-84 | | 1185. | 1209. | A | |
| 11-23-84 | 1220. | | 1196. | B | |
| 12- 3-84 | | 1182. | 1206. | | |
| 12- 7-84 | | 1163. | 1187. | C | 2 |
| 12-18-84 | 1212. | | | | |

## Minute Wave Chart For Intermediate Wave 4
### Showing A,B,C Reactions

| Date | Close New Highs | Close New Lows | Direction Reversal Price | Minor Wave Count | Intermediate Wave Count |
|------|-----------------|----------------|--------------------------|------------------|-------------------------|
| 7-19-85 | 1360. | | 1336. | 5 | 3 |
| 8- 6-85 | | 1325. | 1349. | | |
| 8-12-85 | | 1314. | 1338. | | |
| 8-19-85 | | 1313. | 1337. | A | |
| 9- 9-85 | 1339. | | 1315. | B | |
| 9-11-85 | | 1319. | 1343. | | |
| 9-12-85 | | 1312. | 1336. | | |
| 9-13-85 | | 1308. | 1332. | | |
| 9-17-85 | | 1298. | 1322. | C | 4 |

185

On January 7, 1986 the Dow Jones Industrials closed at $1565.71 (1566). The following day, January 8, the Dow dropped 39.10 points in one day to close at $1526.61.

This was at the time the *largest* single day loss in Stock Market recorded history. This loss caused *great* concern among many, and raised fears that a ''crash'' could be in the making.

However, anyone applying this system of wave counting had *no* problem at all seeing that we have merely entered into Minor Wave 2 (of Intermediate Wave 5).

Following is the Minute Wave chart for Minor Wave 2:

| Date | Close New Highs | Close New Lows | Direction Reversal Price | Minute Wave Count $24.00 | Minor Wave Count $38.00 | Intermediate Wave Count |
|---|---|---|---|---|---|---|
| 1- 7-86 | 1566. | | 1542. | | | |
| 1- 8-86 | | 1527. | 1551. | | | |
| 1- 9-86 | | 1518. | 1542. | | | |
| 1-10-86 | | 1514. | 1538. | A | | |
| 1-16-86 | 1542. | | 1518. | B | | |
| 1-21-86 | | 1515. | 1539. | | | |
| | | | | | 2 | 5 |

## Bull Market (Cont'd)
## 7-24-84 to 8-24-87

| Date | Close New Highs | Close New Lows | Direction Reversal Price | Minor Wave Count | Intermediate Wave Count |
|---|---|---|---|---|---|
| 2-10-86 | 1626. | | 1564. | | |
| 2-12-86 | 1630. | | 1568. | | |
| 2-13-86 | 1645. | | 1583. | | |
| 2-14-86 | 1664. | | 1602. | | |
| 2-18-86 | 1679. | | 1617. | | |
| 2-21-86 | 1698. | | 1636. | | |
| 2-27-86 | 1714. | | 1652. | | |
| 3-11-86 | 1746. | | 1684. | | |
| 3-13-86 | 1754. | | 1692. | | |
| 3-14-86 | 1793. | | 1731. | | |
| 3-20-86 | 1804. | | 1742. | | |
| 3-26-86 | 1811. | | 1749. | | |
| 3-27-86 | 1822. | | 1760. | 3 | |
| 4- 4-86 | | 1739. | 1801. | | |
| 4- 7-86 | | 1736. | 1798. | 4 | |
| 4-14-86 | 1805. | | 1743. | | |
| 4-15-86 | 1810. | | 1748. | | |
| 4-16-86 | 1845. | | 1783. | | |
| 4-17-86 | 1855. | | 1793. | | |
| 4-21-86 | 1856. | | 1794. | 5 | 3 |
| 4-30-86 | | 1784. | 1846. | | |
| 5- 1-86 | | 1778. | 1840. | | |
| 5- 2-86 | | 1775. | 1837. | | |
| 5-16-86 | | 1760. | 1822. | | |
| 5-19-86 | | 1758. | 1858. | A,B,C | |
| 5-28-86 | 1878. | | 1778. | | |
| 5-29-86 | 1882. | | 1782. | | |
| 6- 6-86 | 1886. | | 1786. | | |
| 6-30-86 | 1893. | | 1793. | | |
| 7- 1-86 | 1904. | | 1804. | | |
| 7- 2-86 | 1909. | | 1809. | 1 | |
| 7-14-86 | | 1793. | 1893. | | |
| 7-15-86 | | 1769. | 1869. | | |
| 7-29-86 | | 1767. | 1867. | | |
| 8- 1-86 | | 1764. | 1864. | 2 | |
| 8-18-86 | 1870. | | 1770. | | |
| 8-20-86 | 1881. | | 1781. | | |
| 8-22-86 | 1888. | | 1788. | | |
| 8-26-86 | 1904. | | 1804. | | |
| 8-27-86 | 1905. | | 1805. | | |
| 9- 4-86 | 1920. | | 1820. | 3 | |

the b Wave here occurred during the intra-day trading on May 14, posting a $23.00 gain on the close of 1808.00

Because of the strength of this Bull Market and since the loss on Intermediate Wave 4 was so near the next highest dollar value of $100, we shall at this point again raise the Minor Wave value amount.

## Bull Market (Cont'd)
### 7-24-84 to 8-24-87

| Date | Close New Highs | Close New Lows | Direction Reversal Price | Minor Wave Count | Intermediate Wave Count |
|---|---|---|---|---|---|
| 9-11-86 | | 1793. | 1893. | | |
| 9-12-86 | | 1759. | 1859. | | |
| 9-29-86 | | 1755. | 1855. | 4. | ...although the total loss on Minor Wave 4 amounted to more than the $162.00 value for waves on the Intermediate Wave level—this *was* very close to that amount and it was still on the 4th Minor Wave. We knew that the 5th Wave was yet to come and we had not yet reached the peak of this great Bull Market..... |
| 10-30-86 | 1878. | | 1778. | | |
| 11- 3-86 | 1894. | | 1794. | | |
| 11- 5-86 | 1899. | | 1799. | | |
| 11-24-86 | 1906. | | 1806. | | |
| 11-25-86 | 1912. | | 1812. | | |
| 11-26-86 | 1917. | | 1817. | | |
| 12- 2-86 | 1956. | | 1856. | | |
| 1- 5-87 | 1971. | | 1871. | | |
| 1- 6-87 | 1975. | | 1875. | | |
| 1- 7-87 | 1994. | | 1894. | | |
| 1- 8-87 | 2002. | | 1902. | | |
| 1- 9-87 | 2006. | | 1906. | | |
| 1-12-87 | 2009. | | 1909. | | |
| 1-13-87 | 2013. | | 1913. | | |
| 1-14-87 | 2035. | | 1935. | | |
| 1-15-87 | 2071. | | 1971. | | |
| 1-16-87 | 2077. | | 1977. | | |
| 1-19-87 | 2103. | | 2003. | | |
| 1-20-87 | 2104. | | 2004. | | |
| 1-22-87 | 2146. | | 2046. | | |
| 1-27-87 | 2150. | | 2050. | | |
| 1-28-87 | 2163. | | 2063. | | |
| 2- 2-87 | 2179. | | 2079. | | |
| 2- 4-87 | 2191. | | 2091. | | |
| 2- 5-87 | 2201. | | 2101. | | |
| 2-17-87 | 2237. | | 2137. | | |
| 2-18-87 | 2238. | | 2138. | | |
| 2-19-87 | 2244. | | 2144. | | |
| 3- 4-87 | 2257. | | 2157. | | |
| 3- 5-87 | 2276. | | 2176. | | |
| 3- 6-87 | 2280. | | 2180. | | |
| 3-17-87 | 2285. | | 2185. | | |
| 3-18-87 | 2287. | | 2187. | | |
| 3-19-87 | 2300. | | 2200. | | |
| 3-20-87 | 2334. | | 2234. | | |
| 3-23-87 | 2364. | | 2264. | | |
| 3-24-87 | 2369. | | 2269. | | |
| 3-26-87 | 2373. | | 2273. | | |
| 4- 3-87 | 2390. | | 2290. | | |
| 4- 6-87 | 2405. | | 2305. | 5 | |

## Bull Market (Cont'd)
## 7-24-84 to 8-24-87

| Date | Close New Highs | Close New Lows | Direction Reversal Price | Minor Wave Count | Intermediate Wave Count |
|---|---|---|---|---|---|
| 4-13-87 | | 2287. | 2387. | | |
| 4-14-87 | | 2253. | 2353. | | |
| 4-24-87 | | 2235. | 2335. | ext. 6 | |
| 6- 4-87 | 2337. | | 2237. | | |
| 6- 8-87 | 2352. | | 2252. | | |
| 6- 9-87 | 2353. | | 2253. | | |
| 6-10-87 | 2354. | | 2254. | | |
| 6-11-87 | 2360. | | 2260. | | |
| 6-12-87 | 2378. | | 2278. | | |
| 6-15-87 | 2392. | | 2292. | | |
| 6-16-87 | 2407. | | 2307. | ext. 7... | |
| 6-18-87 | 2408. | | 2308. | | |
| 6-19-87 | 2421. | | 2321. | | |
| 6-22-87 | 2446. | | 2346. | | |
| 6-25-87 | 2451. | | 2351. | | |
| 7- 8-87 | 2464. | | 2364. | | |
| 7-14-87 | 2481. | | 2381. | | |
| 7-15-87 | 2484. | | 2384. | | |
| 7-16-84 | 2497. | | 2397. | | |
| 7-17-87 | 2510. | | 2410. | | |
| 7-28-87 | 2520. | | 2420. | | |
| 7-29-87 | 2540. | | 2440. | | |
| 7-30-87 | 2567. | | 2467. | | |
| 7-31-87 | 2572. | | 2472. | | |
| 8- 6-87 | 2594. | | 2494. | | |
| 8-10-87 | 2636. | | 2536. | | |
| 8-11-87 | 2680. | | 2580. | | |
| 8-13-87 | 2691. | | 2591. | | |
| 8-17-87 | 2701. | | 2601. | | |
| 8-20-87 | 2707. | | 2607. | | |
| 8-21-87 | 2709. | | 2609. | | |
| 8-25-87 | 2722. | | 2622. | | 5 |
| 9- 2-87 | | 2602. | 2702. | | |
| 9- 3-87 | | 2599. | 2699. | | |
| 9- 4-87 | | 2561. | 2661. | | |
| 9- 8-87 | | 2545. | 2645. | | |
| 9-16-87 | | 2530. | 2630. | | |
| 9-17-87 | | 2528. | 2628. | | |
| 9-18-87 | | 2525. | 2625. | a | A |
| 9-21-87 | | 2493. | 2593. | | |

********* LOSS TO THIS POINT EXCEEDS $200.00 THIS SIGNALS THE END OF THE BULL MARKET !!!!!!!

# Addendum

As one can see by going over the current Dow Jones Industrials, the peak of the Bull Market occurred on August 25, 1987 at $2722.00. Using the Price Spiral System, we entered the current Bear Market on September 2, when the Dow dropped to $2602. We then received a further confirmation when the Dow continued to drop past the dollar value ratio of $162.00 on September 21. We had proof positive that we were now beginning the Bear move and were way ahead of most others with this knowledge. Our market positions were switched well before the now infamous "BLACK MONDAY" of October 19, when the Dow fell 508 points in one day. The day that everyone else learned the great Bull had indeed come to its end, with huge financial losses for so many.

Which now brings us to the present time, and the question "What can we now expect?" The answer, I feel is that the market will assume a sideways movement until after the November election, then it will continue its downward move to the end of Intermediate Wave C. Remember, we still have a long way to go until the Bear Market end at the bottom of Wave E. But we have the means and the knowledge with the Price Spiral System to feel confident that we shall indeed be able to track this Bear move with complete accuracy through all of its movements up and down to its very end.

## Current Bear Market

| Date | Close New Highs | Close New Lows | Direction Reversal Price | Minor Wave Count | Intermediate Wave Count |
|---|---|---|---|---|---|
| 8-25-87 | 2722. | | 2622. ......... Bull Market Top ......... | | |
| 9- 2-87 | | 2602. | 2702. | | |
| 9- 3-87 | | 2599. | 2699. | | |
| 9- 4-87 | | 2561. | 2661. | | |
| 9- 8-87 | | 2545. | 2645. | 1 | |
| 9-16-87 | | 2530. | 2630. ********* (Wave 2 occurred during the | | |
| 9-17-87 | | 2528. | 2628. inter-day trading 9/9 to 9/14/87) | | |
| 9-18-87 | | 2525. | 2625. | | |
| 9-21-87 | | 2493. | 2593. ********** 3 ******* *Note*** The loss | | |
| 9-28-87 | 2602. | | 2502. at this point | | |
| 10- 1-87 | 2639. | | 2539. exceeds $200.00, | | |
| 10 2-87 | 2641. | | 2541. 4 giving us *con-* | | |
| 10- 8-87 | | 2517. | 2617. *firmation* that | | |
| 10- 9-87 | | 2482. | 2582. the *Bull Market* | | |
| 10-12-87 | | 2471. | 2571. has *ended.* | | |
| 10-14-87 | | 2413. | 2513. | | |
| 10-15-87 | | 2355. | 2455. | | |
| 10-16-87 | | 2247. | 2347. | | |
| 10-19-87 | | 1739. | 1839. | 5 | A |
| 10-20-87 | 1841. | | 1741. | | |
| 10-21-87 | 2028. | | 1928. | a | |
| 10-26-87 | | 1794. | 1894. | b | |
| 10-29-87 | 1938. | | 1838. | | |
| 10-30-87 | 1994. | | 1894. | | |
| 11- 3-87 | 2014. | | 1914. | c retracement | |
| 11- 9-87 | | 1900. | 2000. | | |
| 11-11-87 | | 1899. | 1999. | | |
| 11-19-87 | | 1885. | 1985. | | |
| 11-30-87 | | 1834. | 1934. | | |
| 12- 3-87 | | 1777. | 1877. | | |
| 12- 4-87 | | 1767. | 1867. | d retracement | |
| 12-11-87 | 1867. | | 1767. | | |
| 12-14-87 | 1933. | | 1833. | | |
| 12-15-87 | 1941. | | 1841. | | |
| 12-16-87 | 1974. | | 1874. | | |
| 12-18-87 | 1975. | | 1875. | | |
| 12-21-87 | 1990. | | 1890. | | |
| 12-23-87 | 2005. | | 1905. | | |
| 1- 4-88 | 2015. | | 1915. | | |
| 1 5-88 | 2032. | | 1932. | | |
| 1- 6-88 | 2038. | | 1938. | | |
| 1- 7-88 | 2052. | | 1952. | | |

## Current Bear Market

| Date | Close New Highs | Close New Lows | Direction Reversal Price | Minor Wave Count | Intermediate Wave Count |
|---|---|---|---|---|---|
| 1- 8-88 | | 1911. | 2011. | ex.f | **** |
| 2-19-88 | 2015. | | 1915. | | |
| 2-23-88 | 2039. | | 1939. | | |
| 2-24-88 | 2040. | | 1940. | | |
| 3- 1-88 | 2072. | | 1972. | | |
| 3- 8-88 | 2081. | | 1981. | | |
| 3-17-88 | 2086. | | 1986. | | |
| 3-18-88 | 2087. | | 1987. | ext. g | |
| 3-25-88 | | 1979. | 2079. | | |
| 3-30-88 | | 1978. | 2078. | ext. h | **** |
| 4- 8-88 | 2090. | | 1990. | | |
| 4-11-88 | 2096. | | 1996. | | |
| 4-12-88 | 2110. | | 2010. | ext. i | |
| 4-14-88 | | 2006. | 2106. | | |
| 4-19-86 | | 1999. | 2099. | | |
| 4-21-88 | | 1987. | 2087. | | |
| 5-12-87 | | 1968. | 2068. | | |
| 5-18-88 | | 1951. | 2051. | | |
| 5-23-88 | | 1941. | 2041. | ext. j | **** |
| 6- 1-88 | 2064. | | 1964. | | |
| 6- 3-88 | 2071. | | 1971. | | |
| 6- 6-88 | 2075. | | 1975. | | |
| 6- 8-88 | 2103. | | 2003. | | |
| 6-14-88 | 2124. | | 2024. | | |
| 6-15-88 | 2131. | | 2031. | | |
| 6-22-88 | 2151. | | 2051. | | |
| 7- 5-88 | 2159. | | 2059. | ext.k | |
| 7-27-88 | | 2054. | 2154. | | |
| 8- 9-88 | | 2034. | 2134. | | |
| 8-15-88 | | 2004. | 2104. | | |

**** Please note the above marked extensions did not drop to the Intermediate level of $162.00, which would have signaled the end of the B wave.